PEKING OPERA PAINTED FACES
—WITH NOTES ON 200 OPERAS

Text by Zhao Menglin and Yan Jiqing
Drawings by Zhao Menglin

MORNING GLORY PUBLISHERS
BEIJING · 1994

Editing, design and layout: Sun Jie
Photographer: Wu Yinbo and Zhang Zudao
English translation: Gong Lizeng
English text editor: Wang Xingzheng
Technical Editor: Yu Shenquan

First edition 1992
Reprinted 1994
ISBN7 − 5054 − 0412 − 1/J · 0132

Published by **MORNING GLORY PUBLISHERS**
— A subsidiary of China International Book Trading Corporation

35 Chegongzhuang Xilu, Beijing 100044, China

Distributed by **CHINA INTERNATIONAL BOOK TRADING CORPORATION**
P.O.Box 399, Beijing
35 Chegongzhuang Xilu, Beijing 100044, China

Printed in the People's Republic of China

七年级家庭作业：The 5th China Beijing Opera Art Festival

jīng jù
第5届中国京剧艺术节

上网查关于京剧的历史发展（history & development）、艺术特点（artistic features）、表现手法（expressions）、分类（type）、伴奏乐器、著名剧目（famous plays）、影响（influence）。每人做一张向别人介绍京剧的海报 poster，海报上要有介绍京剧的短文 short essay。

要求：1，字要写清楚，写一行空一行。

2，至少3段，每段5个句子，每段3个连词。

3，写在有横线的纸上，10/15号交 due。

CONTENTS

PEKING OPERA PAINTED FACES

Lian Po in *Reconciliation of the General and the Minister.*

Xiang Yu in *The Prince Bids Farewell to His Favorite.*

Bao Zheng in
*The Ungrateful
Husband.*

"Stealing the Hal-
berds," an act in
Battle of Wancheng.

Cheng Ziming in *Three Bouts with Tao Sanchun*.

 ou Erdun in
*ealing the
mperial Steed*.

Dian Wei in *Battle
of Wancheng*

Erlang God in *Presenting a Pearl at Rainbow Bridge*.

Monster Spirit in *Havoc in Heaven*.

FOREWORD

$\mathcal{T}$he term "painted face" as used in this book refers to the colorful facial make-up of an actor in traditional Chinese drama. Such make-up is worn mostly by actors playing roles known as *jing* (painted faces) and *chou* (clowns). It is stylized in form, color, and pattern to symbolize the characteristics of specific roles, so that a knowledgeable audience, seeing a painted face, can tell easily whether it is a hero or a villain, a wise man or a fool, to be loved or hated, respected or ridiculed. Thus the painted face is quite appropriately called "a mirror of the soul."

Painted faces were not created by the fancy of some individual. They are the creations of generations of dramatic artists, based on their observations and life experience and their analyses of the *dramatis personae*. According to historical records, the painted face evolved from the merging of two earlier forms of facial disguise or decoration used in theatrical performances: the mask worn by the *daimian* (a *jing*- type role) in a dance of the Tang dynasty (618-907) and the *tumian* ("smeared face") of the sub-*jing* role in Canjun opera, a kind of satirical drama popular in the Tang and Song (960-1279) dynasties.

In 1988 Wong Ouhong, a theorist on Chinese drama, presented a paper at a forum held during an Exhibition of Painted Faces in Chinese Drama. We reprint below some passages that touch on the development of the painted face.

"The embryo of the painted face in Chinese drama was the primitive totem. Over time, this totem evolved into a mask worn by dancers in sacrificial ceremonies to the Exorcist God during the Spring and Autumn period. Thereafter, it developed successively into the *daimian* ('substitute face,' a more elaborate kind of mask) of the Han and Tang, the *tumian* ('smeared face') of the Song and Yuan, and the *lianpu* (painted face, or literally 'face pattern') of the Ming and Qing.

"The painted face, however, did not fully replace the mask on the Chinese stage. Both are still used. The most obvious examples are in the opera to the earth god (*di* opera) in Guizhou, opera to the exorcist god (*nuo* opera) in Jiangxi and Anhui, and in various Tibetan operas, in which all role types wear masks. In one performance several dozen or over a hundred masks may be used.

"In southern *kunqu* opera impersonators of deities and ghosts wear masks instead of painting their faces. Even Peking opera, now a major dramatic form in China, which has contributed greatly to development of the painted face, has retained the masks worn by the God of Official Promotion, God of Wealth, God of Literature, God of the Earth, and God of Thunder. Through use of the mask and/or painted face and the development of facial designs from simple to complex, one may trace the successive stages in the development of Chinese drama."

Although Peking opera has a history of barely two hundred years, it has developed faster than other, older forms of Chinese drama and is more firmly rooted in the masses. Its fascinating painted faces have a special place among the numerous kinds of facial make-up in Chinese drama. Audiences consider them "living art" — as alive as the opera actors themselves.

The Peking opera painted face is characterized by symbolism and exaggeration, that is, by the use of signs and symbols and exaggerated or distorted features to represent a person's character or attributes. Very often eyes, brows, and cheeks are depicted like bats, butterflies, or swallows' wings which, together with an exaggerated mouth and nose, produce the desired facial expressions. An optimistic person is usually portrayed with clear eyes and smooth brows, while a grief-stricken or cruel person will have half-closed eyes and wrinkled brows.

In order to carry on and further develop our rich cultural heritage, we have compiled this book of Peking opera painted faces, which we hope will be of interest to lovers of traditional Chinese opera and a useful reference to students of the fine arts.

From a very large collection of painted-face patterns we have selected 272, including both traditional make-up and new patterns created for newly written operas. Our selections were not limited to any particular school or style, the stress being instead on the quality and popularity of the patterns. A few less common patterns have also been included because they possess certain distinctive characteristics. Basically, the patterns are listed in chronological order following events described in the operas and the lives of the characters impersonated. Insofar as is possible, faces with similar symbolic features have been grouped together to make it easier for readers to study them.

Any study of the painted faces in Peking opera should be made in conjunction with a study of the opera stories, the *dramatis personae*, and the costumes and performances of the actors. For this purpose, we have included a number of pictures drawn by the author showing Peking opera actors in costume and with facial make-up. This will help readers understand, among other things, how Peking opera painted faces are categorized.

All the pictures of painted faces in this book are full, frontal views, which is a departure from the usual practice of giving only partial views. While this new approach is more difficult, it makes it easier for readers to examine the details of a face.

In the process of compiling this book the author has consulted Hao Shouchen's *Collection of Painted Face Patterns,* Wong Ouhong's *Talks on the Painted Face,* Tao Junqi's *A Preliminary Survey of Peking Opera Repertoire,* and other books and manuscripts. In addition, we wish to thank Mr. Sun Changzu for his generous assistance and advice, which were a great encouragement to the author.

We know our own limits and hope all dramatists, dramatic artists, and lovers of Peking opera painted faces will offer comments and opinions on our work.

Peking Opera Painted Faces

I. Origin and Development

The development of the art of painting faces is closely related to that of Chinese dramatic art, although the earliest painted faces, or their precursors, appeared long before Chinese drama took shape. Clowns with a big white spot painted on their faces were seen in Song dynasty operettas and Yuan dynasty poetic dramas of the twelfth and thirteenth centuries. Facial make-up like that of Peking opera *jing* roles (warriors or robust male characters) had, however, been used in songs and dances nearly a thousand years earlier. As far back as the Northern and Southern Dynasties and the Sui-Tang (420-907) a song and dance featured warriors wearing masks, a precursor of the painted face. This is told in the *Old History of the Tang Dynasty: Chapter on Music:* "Prince Lanling of the Northern Qi was a great warrior but had a pretty, womanish face. To frighten his enemies, he would wear a fearsome mask when he went to war. Once, in a battle with the state of Zhou outside Jinyong City, he proved himself the strongest and bravest of all. His people were so proud of him that they composed a song and dance called 'Prince Lanling at the Front' in which the actors wore masks and their movements simulated the way the prince vanquished his enemies." Thus the custom of actors wearing masks began. Though not in general use nowadays, masks are still worn in some traditional operas, such as the local dramas performed by the Bouyei people of Xingyi, Guizhou Province. Such masks may be regarded as living fossils in the history of opera facial make-up.

As Chinese dramatic art developed, the drawbacks of wearing masks became increasingly evident, for masks prevented the actors from showing their facial expressions. A vividly painted face, however, enables audiences to see expressions clearly even from a distance, a great advantage in the days when dramatic performances were usually staged in the open air before large crowds. So actors began to apply powder, ink, paint, and soot to their faces, creating the art of facial make-up.

In the beginning only three sharply contrasting colors — red, white, and black — were generally used in facial make-up. Eyes, ears, nose, mouth, and facial contours were delineated clearly, and a character's most distinctive features, such as thick brows, large eyes, upturned nose, or wide mouth, were usually exaggerated. The earliest painted faces were simple and crude, but with time the designs became more elaborate and ornamental. By the late eighteenth and early nineteenth centuries, when Peking opera had acquired its unique artistic style and methods of performance, the art of Peking opera facial make-up was developing fast, thanks to the improvements and innovations made by successive generations of performers and artists and to the assimilation of the best make-up used in various local operas. Colors and designs have since become richer and more diversified; distinctions between different roles and characters have become sharper, and a host of new faces has been created for both historical and legendary figures.

II. Facial Colors

The basic colors in modern Peking opera painted faces are red, purple (or crimson), black, white, blue, green, yellow, pink, gray, gold, and silver. Originally, colors were used just to emphasize or exaggerate a person's natural complexion. Gradually colors acquired symbolic meanings. In general, red is the color of loyalty and courage; purple, of wisdom, bravery, and steadfastness; black, of loyalty and integrity; watery white, of cruelty and treachery; oily white, of an inflated, domineering person; blue, of valor and resolution; green, of chivalry; yellow, of brutality; dark red, of a loyal, time-tested warrior; and gray, of an old scoundrel. Gold and silver are used on the faces and bodies of deities, Buddhas, spirits, and demons, because their sheen produces a supernatural effect.

Although these symbolic meanings are fairly well established, they are not hard and fast. Great flexibility is allowed in the use of color. For example, in operas based on the *Romance of the Three Kingdoms* the face of the old warrior Guan Yu is painted red to symbolize his courage and loyalty to his elder brother, the king of Shu. But in the opera *Famen Temple* the face of the eunuch Liu Jin is painted red for quite a different purpose: to exaggerate the man's ruddy complexion and mark him as one who holds great power in the imperial court and has lived a life of ease and affluence. His brows, eyes, and mouth are all depicted in a way that betrays his treacherous nature, enabling audiences to recognize him instantly as a scoundrel and despot.

The face of Chao Gai, an outlaw chief in *Outlaws of the Marsh*, is another example of the variant uses of a color. Chao Gai wears a three-tile (see III.2) face of faded yellow, but the yellow does not have its usual meaning of cruelty or brutality, neither of which is an attribute of this outlaw chief. It merely represents the man's natural pale complexion. The red spot painted conspicuously between the eyebrows symbolizes a hero who has joined a good cause.

A dictum familiar to most Peking opera fans, "No red for the three Gangs," illustrates how colors represent human character. The three Gangs (Li Gang, Yao Gang, and Xue Gang) were bold and obstinate, but in Peking operas they are portrayed as solemn and serious, so no red is allowed in their facial make-up, not even on their lips, and no pink powder (which symbolizes humor) is applied to their cheeks. By contrast, in operas adapted from the *Romance of the Yang Family* the cheeks of the two characters Meng Liang and Jiao Zan are powdered pink because these two men are humorous by nature. In *Hongyang Cave*, however, the two no longer have pink cheeks, for this opera portrays them as old people whose temperaments have changed.

In summary, colors are used to symbolize human nature in Peking opera. The choice of colors, largely empirical, is based on the experience of many generations of veteran dramatic artists, through whom a fairly complete set of Peking opera facial patterns has been created.

Fig. 1: Guan Yu in *Drowning the Seven Armies*.

Fig. 2: Bao Zheng in *The Ungrateful Husband*.

III. Types of Painted Faces

It is easy to be confused, perhaps mystified, by the seemingly endless variation in the facial make-up of Peking opera characters. Actually, despite their riot of colors and strong decorative value, there are only about a dozen types of painted faces, but through borrowing and interchanging details many subtypes have been created. These subtypes are based on the physical and mental characteristics of the *dramatis personae*. Because of differences in temperament, the lines and colors in the facial make-up of characters of the same role type are executed differently. Inasmuch as every character possesses individuality, no two painted faces are exactly alike.

    1. Full face. This is a very common type of painted face, so called presumably because more

Fig. 3: Cao Cao in *A Meeting of the Elite*.

Fig. 4: Jiang Wei in *Iron-Cage Mountain*.

than any of the other types it resembles a full human face with all its natural features. The first step is to apply a coat of paint over the entire face to serve as the principal color and to exaggerate the natural complexion. Next, the eyes, brows, nose, mouth, and tiny wrinkles are delineated to produce the desired facial expression. The brushwork is like tracing lines in Chinese painting, using precise, steady, and vigorous strokes.

Guan Yu's facial make-up (Fig. 1) in the opera *Drowning the Seven Armies* is a red full face. It gives the old warrior a solemn and dignified appearance.

Judge Bao Zheng's make-up (Fig. 2) in *The Ungrateful Husband* is a black full face. The white knitted brows symbolize loyalty to country and concern for the welfare of the people, underscoring the judge's ironclad integrity and strict observance of the law. The white crescent in the middle of the forehead is a symbol of the mysterious powers possessed by this judge, who

Fig. 5: Dou Erdun in *Stealing the Imperial Steed.*

Fig. 6: Yao Qi in *Grass-Bridge Pass.*

tries cases in the upper world by day and in the netherworld at night.

A white powdered full face with eyes, ears, nose, mouth, and facial expressions delineated in black symbolizes a detestable character — a traitor, tyrant, or despot. An example of this is Cao Cao's make-up (Fig. 3) in *A Meeting of the Elite,* in which he is portrayed as a dual personality: suspicious, deceitful, and scheming on the one hand and very capable militarily and politically on the other. The prime features of his make-up are a layer of white powder that symbolically masks the evil side of the man's nature and long, thin three-corner eyes with lines at the corners that represent craftiness.

In some full faces the paint is rubbed on with the fingers or some soft material. A face made up in this way does not symbolize anything and is generally used for a supporting role. Its style and facial expression are relatively simple.

Fig. 7: Zhang Fei in *Reed Marsh*.

Fig. 8: Xu Yanzhao in *Second Entry into the Palace*.

2. Three-tile face, also called three-pit face. This is a variation of the full face. The eyes, brows, and nose are exaggerated or enlarged by the addition of two eye sockets and a nose pit, represented as three irregularly shaped patches of color called "tiles," though they bear little resemblance to roof tiles. It is a widely used type of painted face characterized by symmetry of design, varied colors, and meticulous brushwork, like a *gongbi* painting. It embodies all the basics of Peking opera facial make-up. Subtypes are: upright three-tile face, pointed three-tile face, flowered three-tile face, and old or faded three-tile face.

The upright three-tile face is used largely to represent a loyal and courageous warrior. Its distinguishing features are near-vertical brows, large eyes, a round nose pit, and a full beard covering the mouth. The usual colors are red, white, and purple. Jiang Wei's make-up (Fig. 4) in *Iron Cage Mountain* is an example of a red upright three-tile face. The *taijitu* (diagram of a cosmological scheme) on his forehead is to show that he was a disciple of Zhuge Liang, prime minister of the kingdom of Shu, and like his teacher is a man of great ability with profound knowledge of the universe.

The pointed three-tile face is usually distinguished by arched or pointed brows, raised or slanting eyes, and a pointed nose pit. The beard may be a full one covering the mouth or a shorter one (called *zha*) that leaves the mouth exposed. The usual colors are red, white, blue, purple, and yellow. This face may be worn by very different characters: a bold, reckless warrior or a despot.

The flowered three-tile face has intricate, variegated designs around the eyes, brows, and nose. Basically, however, the face consists of three large patches, or "tiles." The beard is usually red or black with the mouth exposed; sometimes the character wears only a bar-shaped mustache. This kind of painted face is worn by a bold warrior or a greenwood hero. Dou Erdun wears a blue flowered three-tile face (Fig. 5) in *Stealing the Imperial Steed*. The sharp pointed figure between the brows represents the deadly two-hook weapon he uses so deftly.

The old or faded three-tile face is for a very old person, who may be a positive or a negative character. It is always used with a full white or grayish-black beard. A distinctive feature is sagging lower eyelids, shaped like low-hanging clouds, quite characteristic of old men whose skin and muscles around the eyes tend to slacken. The nose pit is sometimes delineated in black or gray to represent an aged person's grizzled hair.

3. Cross face. This make-up evolved from the three-tile face. The principal color symbolizing the nature of the character is a narrow strip from the top of the forehead to the tip of the nose. This strip intersects the line of the eye sockets to form a cross, hence the name.

The two subtypes—old cross face and variegated cross face—both represent positive characters, such as heroes or bold warriors. The old cross face has a full beard covering the mouth and the variegated face a beard with the mouth exposed. Yao Qi in *Grass-Bridge Pass* has an old black-cross face (Fig. 6). His eyelids droop as a sign of age, but his cheeks are painted pink to show that he still has the vigor of youth. Zhang Fei in *The Reed Marsh* has a variegated black-cross face (Fig. 7). As the bat-shaped brows and smiling eyes resemble a butterfly, the face is also called a butterfly black-cross face.

4. Six-tenth face. This facial make-up, also developed from the full face, is so called because the principal color symbolizing the nature of the character occupies about six tenths of the face. On the forehead, the principal color is applied only on a narrow strip in the center. The rest of the forehead is taken up by enlarged white eyebrows, which occupy about four tenths of the face. Also called an old face, this make-up represents an old and loyal general who has ably served his cause. The principal color may be red, black, or purple, set off by a long, full snowy-white or dark-gray beard. Xu Yanzhao's make-up (Fig. 8) in *Second Entry into the Palace* and Huang Gai's (Face 73) in *A Meeting of the Elite* are examples.

5. Broken-flower face. This make-up evolved from the flowered three-tile face. The principal color is on the forehead. Various designs in other colors are added to other parts of the face. These designs vary in shape and composition and are executed with small, intricate, and broken lines. The face may be clean shaven, or it may wear a bar-shaped mustache or a black or red *zha* beard. It

19

usually represents a greenwood outlaw or a rough and uncouth warrior, who may be a positive or a negative character. Li Kui's make-up in *The Black Whirlwind* is a black broken-flower face. The nose pit is painted in full to indicate that the man is square as well as brave. Ma Wu wears a blue or green broken-flower face in *Capture of Luoyang*. The brushstrokes are executed meticulously to convey the idea that this rough and uncouth greenwood hero is meticulous at times. Yang Yansi, the seventh son in *Golden Sand Dune,* also wears a black broken-flower face. The Chinese character for "tiger," written in cursive script on the forehead, signifies the man's peerless courage.

6. Slanting (or asymmetric) face. As the name suggests, this is a rather uncomely make-up used chiefly to represent a thug or an accomplice in a crime. The facial features are painted asymmetrically, the idea being that the character is a dishonest person who will use devious means to gain an end. The composition is based on that of broken-flower and three-tile faces; a great variety of colors is used, and the face may be clean shaven or wear a *zha* beard. In special cases a slanting face may represent a positive role. A notable example is Zheng Ziming in *Execution of the Yellow Robe*. In his youth Zheng Ziming had saved a man from being killed by an orangutan, but in doing so his own face was mauled by the beast. Therefore he is portrayed with a black broken-flower slanting face to symbolize scars. Another example is Zhu Biao in *Three Attacks on Zhu Family Village*, an episode from *Outlaws of the Marsh*. According to the novel, Zhu Biao is a handsome young man, but on the Peking opera stage he is depicted with a disgusting slanting face. His fiance was kidnapped by outlaws of Liangshan, and at the news his face was contorted with rage and anxiety. Apparently the designer of the painted face chose to portray him in this ugly mood.

7. Monk or Taoist face. This make-up is similar to the three-tile face. Its distinguishing features are kidney-shaped eye sockets and floral patterns around the nose pit and mouth. In the center of the forehead is a red pearl-like object or nine dots, signs that the character has been initiated into Buddhist monkhood. The principal color is white, red, yellow, or blue, white being the most common. The face may be clean shaven or have a curly mustache, called *qiu*. Lu Zhishen, the Flower Monk, wears a white monk face in *Wild Boar Forest* and Fatty Huang wears a yellow one with no mustache in *Reconciliation of the Ba and Luo Families*.

A Taoist face is made by joining the two brows or eye sockets of a three-tile face. Pang Tong's make-up in *A Meeting of the Elite* is an example of a purple Taoist face. The man's Taoist identity is represented by a diagram of a cosmological scheme or the Eight Diagrams painted on the forehead.

8. Eunuch face. This make-up represents a eunuch who tyrannizes people. Only two colors, red and white, are used. The face is basically similar to a full face or a three-tile face, except that certain features indicative of a despot are magnified: thin, pointed brows that suggest craftiness; eye sockets shaped like kitchen knives to symbolize butchery of the people; a beardless mouth turned downward at the corners, a sign of cruelty and deceitfulness; a circle of light on the forehead to mock the eunuch's claim to be a disciple of the Buddha, "cleansed" of all sensual desires because he has been castrated; and lines representing folds on the plump cheeks and forehead, marks of ease and comfort.

Fig. 10: Blue Dragon in *Havoc in Heaven.*

Fig. 9: Monkey Sun Wukong in *Havoc in Heaven.*

9. Ingot face. In this type of make-up the forehead is a different color from the other parts of the face, and a patch across the middle of the face resembles a shoe-shaped gold or silver ingot (used for money in ancient China). Subtypes are: ordinary ingot face, inverted ingot face, and variegated ingot face.

Ordinary ingot face. This is similar to the three-tile face and is used mostly to represent a warrior or general of lower rank.

Inverted ingot face. The face above the brows is red; below, white. The ingot is inverted. Lines expressing the character's moods and feelings are added around the eyes and nose. This face may represent a wicked accomplice to a crime or just a comical, insignificant person.

Variegated ingot face. This make-up has a complicated design somewhat similar to the broken-flower face. Its distinguishing features are the variegated eye sockets and upturned nostrils. The

Fig. 11: Golden Head Fairy in *Five-Flower Cave.*

Fig. 13: Qin Ying in *Golden Water Bridge.*

Fig. 12: Roc in *Lion-and-Camel Ridge.*

principal color is on the forehead, and there is usually a *zha* beard. As this make-up is worn by judges of the netherworld in operas based on myths, it is also called judge face. Sometimes a boorish person with a fierce appearance and a grotesque physique wears such make-up.

10. Symbolic face. This make-up is generally used in operas adapted from fairy tales. As its composition and colors must be based on the image and features of the fairy or monster it represents, there are no fixed patterns. While the make-up should resemble the character portrayed, it should not be too realistic. Most important is to capture the spirit of the subject so that audiences know at a glance what kind of fairy or monster it is. Examples of symbolic faces are the make-up of the Monkey King and Blue Dragon (Figs. 9 and 10) in *Havoc in Heaven,* the Golden Centipede (Fig. 11) in *Five-Flower Cave,* the Great Roc (Fig. 12) in *Lion-and-Camel Ridge,* the god Erlang's dog which barks at heaven (Fig. 15) in *Precious Lotus Lantern,* and Qin Yin, with a

Fig. 15: Dog That Barks at Heaven in *The Magic Lantern.*

Fig. 14: Yang Jian the Erlang God in *Havoc in Heaven.*

pointed mouth and monkey cheeks (Fig. 13), in *Golden Water Ridge.*

11. Fairy face. This make-up, derived from the full face and three-tile face, represents Buddhas and deities. Its composition is patterned on Buddhist images. Gold and silver, the principal colors, symbolize holiness and dignity. Alternatively, gold and silver lines or patches may be added to the background color. A colored ball on a celestial general's helmet distinguishes him from earthly warriors. Apart from these distinguishing features, any unusual mark or trait supposedly possessed by a supernatural being is generally revealed in his stage make-up. For example, the god Erlang Yang Jian (Fig. 14) is said to have three eyes, so a third eye is added on the forehead of his painted face.

12. Clown face, also called three-flower face or little flower face. Caricature is used to produce comical effects. A distinctive feature is a white patch painted over the nose ridge, which may be

Fig. 16: Jiang Gan in *A Meeting of the Elite*.

Fig. 17: Jia Gui in *Famen Temple*.

Fig. 18: Zhu Guangzu in *Chain-Bend Stockade*.

Fig. 19: Chong Gongdao in *Escorting the Woman Prisoner*.

square, round, triangular, or diamond-shaped, depending on the role. The way the eyes, brows, nose, mouth, and facial expressions are depicted also differs. Many very different roles use clown make-up: detestable rogues and lovable children; misers and philanthropists; corrupt officials and upright judges; emperors, kings, officers, down to standard-bearers, mule drivers, and news vendors. Thus there are many kinds of clowns — warrior clowns, civilian clowns, old clowns, wicked clowns, buffoons. Some examples follow:

24

Jiang Gan (Fig. 16), the great blunderer in *A Meeting of the Elite*, is a civilian clown. His make-up reveals an outwardly clever person but actually a foolish pedant. Jia Gui (Fig. 17), a eunuch in *The Famen Temple*, wears the make-up of a buffoon. It represents the characteristic of a low-ranking eunuch: servile and cowardly in the presence of his superiors (not daring to sit down even when told to do so), but arrogant and domineering toward people under him, relying on the power and influence of his master to bully others. Zhu Guangzu (Fig. 18), a character in *Chain-Bend Mountain*, has a warrior clown face, which distinguishes him as an astute, gallant, and chivalrous man. Chong Gongdao (Fig. 19), the old escort in *Escorting the Woman Prisoner*, wears an old clown face, symbolizing a kindhearted man ready to help others.

Many kinds of beards and mustaches are worn by these clowns. Most common are the *yichuo* (a short clipped mustache), *ertiao* (Fig. 18 — a long mustache with upturned ends, somewhat like a handlebar mustache), *chousan* (Fig. 16 — a chin beard and a mustache with downturned ends), *sixi* (whiskers gathered into four tufts), *wucuo* (Fig. 19 — whiskers gathered into five tufts, two forming the chin beard), *badiao* (a mustache shaped like an inverted "V"), and *diaota* (beard hanging down like an inverted pagoda).

13. Heroic face and little demon face. "Heroic" face is not the face of a hero, but of a fighter or a teacher of the martial arts. It is basically the same as the variegated three-tile face, broken-flower face, or slanting face, but the design is simpler and executed more freely.

The little demon face depicts a heavenly warrior or little demon in operas based on myths. It is basically the same as a symbolic face. Both the heroic face and little demon face are worn by supporting roles. Their designs must be simple to distinguish them from the principal characters in an opera.

IV. Symbolic Meanings of Painted Faces

As a person's natural features do not adequately reflect his character or personality, an artist designing the painted face for a certain role in Chinese drama must, for both practical and aesthetic purposes, deliberately exaggerate or distort the most typical features while omitting less important details, so as to bring into sharp focus what best represents his subject's individuality. This is a bold and ingenious way of doing theatrical make-up. It enables audiences to see clearly the distinguishing features and colors on the actor's face from a distance and to enjoy the exquisite beauty of the designs when near. With the addition of appropriate signs and symbols, a painted face can reveal not only physical and physiological features (age, appearance, temperament) but also socially endowed aspects (status, skills, nicknames) and even the articles or weapons a character habitually uses (halberd, hook, bottle gourd, etc.).

Hou Yi was a legendary figure who supposedly shot down nine suns. When he is impersonated on the stage, his facial make-up includes the images of nine suns as a token of this exploit. Similarly, the Big Dipper God has a figure of the Big Dipper painted on his face, and the Fire

1. Cleaning the face and preparing the background.

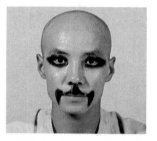

2. Positioning and rubbing in the eye sockets and nose pit.

3. Applying white powder on the background.

4. Filling in the different parts, painting the black eye sockets, adding black lines.

5. Painting a red stripe from top of forehead to top of nose.

6. Finishing touches.

Fig. 20: Process of doing painted faces:

Judge of Hades wears an image of flames. The "grass dragon" on the face of Zhao Kuangyin, first emperor of the Song Dynasty, and the character for "king" on the forehead of Huyan Zan, a Xiongnu chief, are symbols of social status. The lotus flower and peony on the foreheads of Zhong Lichun and Chen Jinding respectively symbolize female warriors. The disfigurements of Sima Shi, his left eye plagued by a tumor, Xiahou Dun, his left eye blinded by an arrow, Li Keyun, his forehead scratched by an eagle, and Zheng Ziming, his face mauled by an orangutan, are all represented on their painted faces. The character for "longevity" between Xiang Yu's brows and his sad-looking eyes, the batlike brows and smiling eyes in Zhang Fei's make-up, the gourd-shaped brows of Meng Liang, orchid-leaf brows of Jiao Zan, "lazy silkworm" brows of Guan Yu, "peacock" brows of Lu Zhishen, "mantis" brows of Yao Gang, suspicious eyes of Cao Cao,

Fig. 21: Process of doing the painted face of Dou Erdun.

and smiling eyes of Niu Gao—all represent some distinguishing feature or quality of the person portrayed.

V. Make-up Techniques

Peking opera facial make-up is a sophisticated art requiring great skill. The brushstrokes must be accurate and forceful, as in painting and calligraphy; the colors must be applied so as to produce the desired shades and tones; and ink for the contours must be used very sparingly. A painted face will possess life and spirit and be appreciated by audiences only when it is executed with skill and care.

Although there is an established pattern for the painted face of almost every Peking opera character, an actor impersonating a certain person is advised not to follow the set pattern too rigidly. He should take into consideration such factors as the shape of his own face, the plot of the opera, and any special conditions or requirements of the performance. Only thus can he successfully represent both the outward features and the inherent traits of the person he is portraying. The famous Peking opera *jing* actor Hao Shoucheng has been acclaimed as a "living Cao Cao" not just because of his excellent impersonation of this famous figure of the Three Kingdoms period; the painted face he created for Cao Cao contributed significantly to his success. Anatomists who have examined and analyzed his stage make-up say that the lines on the forehead of his painted face for Cao Cao virtually coincide with the nerve lines on his own face. In this way, when he portrays Cao Cao in different moods, his facial expressions are more vivid. His painted face is an organic part of his acting.

An experienced actor-artist is able to remedy defects on his face or in his stature by means of facial make-up. A short man or one with a long face, for example, can retouch or redo a painted face to suit his physical conditions. This is what *jing* actors mean when they say, "Facial make-up can change one's form."

The process of facial make-up consists basically of the following steps (see Fig. 20):

1. Cleaning the face and preparing the background;
2. Positioning the different parts of the face and rubbing in the eye sockets and nose pit;
3. Applying white powder on the background;
4. Filling in the different parts, painting the black eye sockets, adding black lines;
5. Painting a red stripe from top of forehead to tip of nose;
6. Finishing touches.

Let us take as an example the blue-flowered three-tile face of Dou Erdun in *Stealing the Imperial Steed* (Fig. 21):

1. Cleaning the face and preparing the background: Wash the face clean, then dip the fingers in a thin solution of white watercolor and rub the face gently and evenly to remove all greasy spots.

2. Positioning the different parts of the face and rubbing in the eye sockets and nose pit: Dip the fingers in a thin solution of blue watercolor and rub the solution on the forehead, nose ridge, and cheeks to show in rough outline their positions on the face. Then dip the fingers in thin black oil and trace the eye sockets and nose pit, leaving space on the eye sockets for the white eyeballs to be added later.

As these two steps are done by the fingers, they are called "finger rubbing."

3. Painting the white base and white lines: This and the following steps are done with a brush. Dip the brush in a thick solution of white watercolor, then do the white lines of the *yintang* (a strip shaped like a gallbladder extending from the top of the nose ridge to the top of the forehead), the white base and lines on the brows, the white lines under the eye sockets, the white base of the nose pit, the white curved mustache flanking the mouth pit, the white circles representing eyeballs on the black eye sockets, and lastly the white chin.

4. Painting the black designs and black lines: Go over the eye sockets with black oil, leaving the

Fig. 22: Former facial make-up
of Lian Po in *Reconciliation of
the General and the Minister.*

Fig. 23: Present facial make-up of Lian Po in
*Reconciliation of the General and
the Minister.*

eyeballs white. Paint the black mouth pit. Then, using a new brush dipped in black ink, do two halberdlike figures on the brows just above the eye sockets and two hooklike figures on the white chin.

5. Painting the red designs: Paint a gall-shaped figure in red oil within the *yintang,* leaving a uniform white border on all sides. Add the upturned nostrils in black, then paint two thin but sturdy red strips on the curves flanking the mouth pit. Lastly, paint the lips and upper parts of the brows red.

6. Adding blue watercolor to the remaining parts of the face and yellow above the brows: Paint the forehead and cheeks with a brush dipped in thick blue watercolor. Add yellow oil to the topmost parts of the brows.

So that movements of the actor's eyes and mouth are clearly visible, the white lines on his brows, below the eye sockets, and on the curves around the nose pit and mouth and the white circles that represent his eyes should not be too thin. The two halberds on the brows represent wrinkles and should not be depicted too realistically. The gall-shaped figure on the *yintang* should be painted conspicuously, for it is a symbol of the prowess of the man who dared to enter the imperial camp at night and steal the emperor's horse.

The art of Peking opera make-up is continually being perfected along with the development of Peking opera itself. An example is the changes in the painted face of the old warrior Lian Po in *Reconciliation of the General and the Minister*. Originally, this warrior wore a purple six-tenths face (Fig. 22). This has now been changed to an "old face," based on the old pink six-tenth face and old three-tile face (Fig. 23). The forehead patch with the principal color has been widened, and the two white brows have been joined to represent knitted brows. With these changes the painted face now symbolizes not only the old warrior's courage and loyalty but also his tendency to worry too much and get himself into an impasse as well as his willingness to correct himself when he knows he is in the wrong. Both dramatic artists and audiences have approved of these changes.

Thus the art of painted faces must not be limited by established patterns and formulas. It is important to progress and improve on the basis of tradition.

Illustra-
tions of
Painted
Faces

5. Wen Zhong

7. Jiang Shang

6. Chong Houhu

8. Chong the Black Tiger

9. Zhongli Chun

11. Li Ke

10. Mao Ben

12. Lei Zhenzi

13. Wei Jiang

15. Ying Kaoshu

14. Xian Mie

16. Tu Angu

17. Xu Jia

19. Zhuan Zhu

18. Ji Liao

20. Mi Nanwa

21. Li Gang

23. Lian Po

22. Yi Li

24. Hu Shang

25. Jing Ke

27. Zhao Gao

26. Wang Ling

28. Xiahou Ying

29. Ying Bu

31. Xiang Yu

30. Peng Yue

32. Lü Matong

33. Yao Qi

35. Wu Han

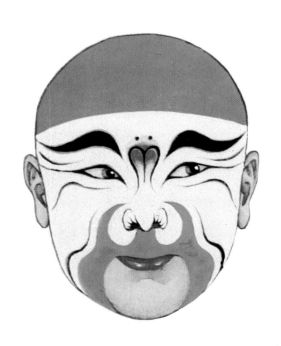

34. Guo Rong

36. Wang Yuan

41

37. Niu Miao

39. Yao Gang

38. Su Xian

40. Ma Wu

41. Zhang Fei

43. Guan Yu

42. Pang Tong

44. Zhou Cang

45. Wei Yan

47. Meng Da

46. Yan Yan

48. Sha Moke

49. Jiang Wei

51. Xiahou De

50. Zhang Bao

52. Deng Ai

53. Cao Cao

55. Dian Wei

54. Xiahou Dun

56. Xiahou Yuan

57. Xu Chu

59. Cao Hong

58. Zhang He

60. Xu Huang

77. Jiang Qing

79. Zhou Tai

78. Ling Tong

80. Zhou Chu

81. Yuchi Baolin

83. Cheng Yaojin

82. Shan Xiongxin

84. Yuchi Gong

85. Jin Jia

87. Tong Huan

86. Li Yuanba

88. Li Mi

54

89. Yang Lin

91. Qin Ying

90. Xin Wenli

92. Dou Yihu

93. Xue Gang

95. Su Baotong

94. Xue Kui

96. An Dianbao

97. Ba Lan

99. He Tianlong

98. Yuwen Chengdu

100. Bao Zi'an

101. Fatty Huang

103. The Orangutan's Courage

102. Gai Suwen

104. Ba Jie

105. Zhu Wen

107. Meng Juehai

106. Li Keyong

108. Hu Li

109. Guo Ziyi

111. Wang Yanzhang

110. Zhou Dewei

112. Yu Hong

113. Zheng Ziming

115. Zhao Kuangyin

114. Huyan Zan

116. Cui Zijian

117. Gao Wang

119. King Tianqing

118. Han Chang

120. Bai Tianzuo

121. Meng Liang

123. Jiao Zan

122. Yang Yande

124. Yang Yansi

63

125. Ba Ruoli

127. Fu Long

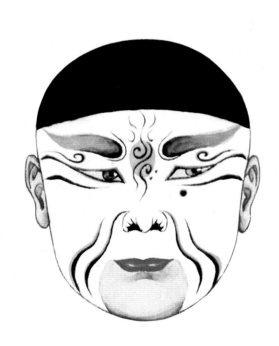

126. Pan Hong

128. Tao Hong

129. Bao Zhen

131. Wang Chao

130. Zhao Hu

132. Ma Han

133. Zhang Tianlong

135. Huyan Qing

134. Boy attendant

136. Wang Wen

137. Han Zhang

139. Lu Fang

138. Xu Qing

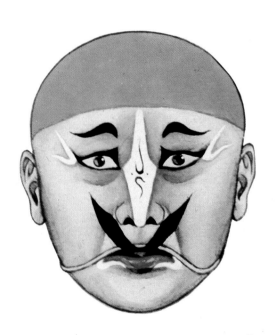

140. Jiang Ping

141. Gongsun Sheng

143. Chao Gai

142. Liu Tang

144. Lu Zhishen

145. Li Kui

147. Bai Sheng

146. Yang Zhi

148. Wang Ying

149. Xuan Zan

151. Qin Ming

150. Huyan Zhuo

152. Su Chao

153. Zhou Tong

155. Tang Long

154. Guan Sheng

156. Yang Lin

157. Zhu Long

159. Luan Tingyu

158. Zhu Hu

160. Zhu Biao

161. Zhang Shun

163. Ni Rong

162. Xu Shiying

164. Shi Qian

165. Gao Deng

167. Gao Qiu

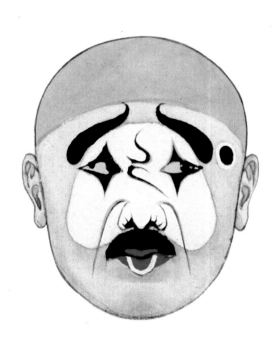

166. Dong Chao

168. Xue Ba

169. Hamichi

171. Chai Gui

170. Jin Chanzi

172. Hei Fengli

173. Niu Gao

175. Di Lei

174. He Yuanqing

176. Wu Zhu

76

177. Li Tingzhi

179. Bo Yan

178. Gold-eyed Monk

180. Silver-eyed Monk

181. Mu Ying

183. Jiang Zhong

182. Xu Yanzhao

184. Chi Fushou

185. Wanyan Long

187. Yan Peiwei

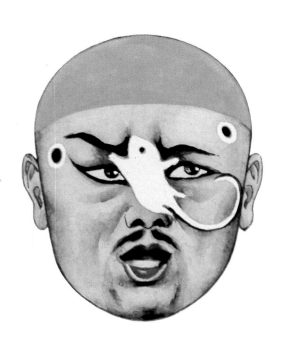

186. Lou Ashu

188. Mother of Hua Yun

189. Li Qi

191. Liu Biao

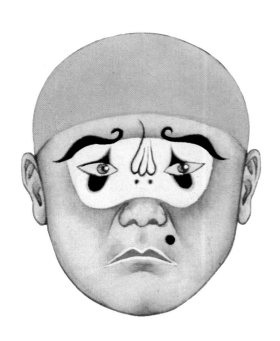

190. Jia Gui

192. Liu Jin

193. Liu Lujing

195. Ben Wu

194. Shen Yanlin

196. De Lu

197. Liu Zongmin

199. Hao Yaoqi

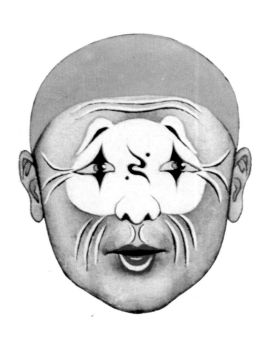

198. Chong Gongdao

200. Xia

82

201. He Tianlong

203. Dou Erdun

202. He Tianbiao

204. Hao Wen

213. Jiao Zhenyuan

215. Wu Tianqiu

214. Hua Delei

216. Li Pei

217. Cai Tianhua

219. Lang Rubao

218. Deng Jiugong

220. Dou Hu

221. God of Wealth

223. Ling Guan

222. Kang Jinlong

224. Ang'ri Ji

225. Jade Emperor

227. Sakyamuni

226. Li the Heavenly King

228. The Great Sage

229. Zhao the Heavenly Sovereign

231. Ma the Heavenly Sovereign

230. Wen the Heavenly Sovereign

232. Liu the Heavenly Sovereign

233. Monster Spirit

235. Erlang God

234. Blue Dragon

236. White Tiger

245. Bull Monster

247. Sandy Wujing

246. Pigsy Bajie

248. Yellow-robed Monster

249. Green Lion

251. White Elephant

250. Cat God

252. Gold-Coin Leopard

253. Peacock

255. Tongque Bird

254. Daytime Parrot

256. Roc

257. Ao Guang

259. Ao Run

258. Lobster General

260. Commander Turtle

261. The Big Dipper

263. Willow Spirit

262. Han Zhongli

264. Jade Hare

98

265. Toad Spirit

267. The Dog That Barks at Heaven

266. Golden-Head Spirit

268. Scorpion Spirit

269. Wei Tuo

271. Taiyi the Immortal

270. Deer Child

272. Crane Child

100

EXPLANATIONS OF
THE PAINTED FACES
WITH NOTES ON
THE OPERAS

1. Zheng Lun with a green pointed three-tile face in *Green Dragon Pass*, an opera based on an episode in the novel *Canonization of the Gods*. This novel, written in the Ming dynasty, tells of the struggles between the rulers of the Shang and Zhou dynasties, but the plots and characters are mostly fictitious. Gods, fairies, and other supernatural beings, fighting each other with magic and magic weapons, dominate many of the stories. The novel begins with the political turmoil that engulfed the last years of the Shang dynasty and the uprising led by King Wu of Zhou and ends with the canonizing of gods by Jiang Ziya, a prime minister of Zhou, and enfeoffment of feudal lords by King Wu. Green Dragon Pass was a strategic spot hotly contested by the Shang and Zhou armies. Zheng Lun was a general under King Wen, the father of King Wu. In the opera he is sent to attack Green Dragon Pass defended by Shang general Qiu Yin. Although not a god, Zheng Lun has the power of exhaling white smoke to conceal himself. His adversary also possesses magic powers, so neither can defeat the other. In the end Zheng Lun captures the pass with the help of the gods.

2. Chen Qi with a red flowered three-tile face in *Green Dragon Pass*. Chen Qi was a grain officer supposedly versed in black magic. He was a subordinate of Qiu Yin, the Shang general who defended Green Dragon Pass.

3. Hou Yi with a purple three-tile face, a leading character in *Chang'e Flees to the Moon*, adapted from *Collected Stories of the Supernatural* by Gan Bao, a scholar and historian of the Eastern Jin dynasty. Most of the stories are about fairies and demons, but there are also some folk legends. Hou Yi was Chang'e's husband. As he was a very cruel man, Chang'e disliked him intensely. According to the story, one day when Hou Yi was drunk, Chang'e swallowed his pills of immortality. When Hou Yi awoke and found the pills gone, he wanted to kill his wife, but the pills had given Chang'e the power to fly and she escaped to the moon.

4. Tuxing Sun, a dwarf with a yellow symbolic face in *Three-Mountain Pass*, adapted from an episode in *Canonization of the Gods*. This dwarf was a general who had the power of penetrating into the earth. He served under Deng Jiugong, a Shang general who guarded Three-Mountain Pass and fought against Jiang Ziya. Deng Jiugong promised to marry his daughter Chanyu to Tuxing Sun someday if he could defeat the Zhou. Later Tuxing Sun was captured by Jiang Ziya, who told him Deng Jiugong's marriage promise was only a trick. Jiang ordered Tuxing Sun to kidnap Chanyu, forced her to marry the dwarf, then sent her over to the Shang camp to persuade her father to surrender, which he did.

5. Wen Zhong with a red six-tenth face, the leading character in *Returning to Court*, an episode in *Canonization of the Gods*. Wen Zhong was the grand tutor in the Shang imperial court. Zhou the last king of the Shang dynasty was a lewd and wicked ruler. Two treacherous court officials, Fei Zhong and You Hun, abetted him in his crimes. When Wen Zhong returned from a successful military expedition to the North Sea and heard of the corruptness of the imperial court, he had the two wicked officials bound and flogged and chastised the king for killing loyal and innocent people.

6. Chong Houhu with a white flowered three-tile face in *Presenting Lady Daji*, an episode in *Canonization of the Gods*. Chong Houhu was one of four feudal lords serving under King Zhou of the Shang dynasty. Su Hu, the governor of Jizhou, had a beautiful daughter

called Daji. The lascivious King Zhou, hearing of her beauty, summoned her father and demanded that she be married to him. When Su Hu refused, the king ordered Chong Houhu to attack Jizhou, forcing Su Hu to yield to his demand. On their way to the capital, the father and daughter put up at an inn. During the night a fox spirit came and swallowed the girl and then assumed her form. King Zhou, unaware of what had happened, married the fox spirit, which turned out to be a very wicked creature. Its wickedness contributed to the eventual downfall of the Shang dynasty.

7. Jiang Shang, or Jiang Ziya, with an old pink full face, the leading character in *Wei River*, adapted from an episode in *Canonization of the Gods*. King Wen of Zhou, seeking capable men to help him establish his dynasty, met Jiang Shang on the banks of the Wei and made him his prime minister.

8. Chong the Black Tiger with a black broken-flower face, a character in *Presenting Lady Daji*. He was the younger brother of Chong Houhu and was the Marquis of Caozhou.

9. Zhongli Chun with a female blue broken-flower face in *The Banquet on the Xiang River*, adapted from *Tales of Heroes and Martyrs*, a historical novel. Zhongli Chun was the wife of King Xuan of Qi of the Spring and Autumn period. In the opera she accompanies her husband to a banquet given by the King of Wei on the bank of the Xiang River. The banquet is a trap to kidnap King Xuan, but the clever Zhongli Chun foils the plot and helps her husband to escape.

10. Mao Ben with a gray broken-flower face in *Five-Thunder Formation*, adapted from *Days of Swords and Daggers*, a historical novel. The opera takes place in the last years of the Warring States period. Wang Jian, a general of Qin, hires a sorcerer called Mao Ben to help him invade the state of Qi. This sorcerer with his magic powers conjures a formidable battle formation known as the Five-Thunder Formation.

11. Li Ke with a black broken butterfly face in *The Trick of the Bees*, adapted from an episode in *New History of the Eastern Zhou*, a long novel revised by Feng Menglong of the Ming dynasty and further revised and annotated by Cai Yuanfang of the Qing. The novel is based on the history of the Spring and Autumn and Warring States periods, which together spanned more than five centuries. It begins in the last years of the Western Zhou and ends with the first Qin emperor's conquest of the six states in 221 BC. Li Ke was an official serving Duke Xian (r. 676-651 BC) of the state of Jin. Duke Xian had a pampered concubine called Li Ji, an ambitious woman who wanted her own son to inherit the dukedom. One day she spread honey on her hair so that a swarm of bees was attracted to it. She asked Shensheng, the duke's rightful heir, to drive away the bees, then accused the young man of taking liberties with her. Unable to extricate himself, Shensheng committed suicide. When Duke Xian died, Li Ke with help from the state of Qin killed Li Ji's sons Xiqi and Zhuozi and made Yiwu, brother of Shensheng, the duke of Jin.

12. Lei Zhenzi with a blue symbolic face in *The One Hundred Sons*, adapted from an episode in *Canonization of the Gods*. Lei Zhenzi was an adoped son of King Wen of the Zhou dynasty. One day when the king was still a marquis, he was summoned to the capital by King Zhou of the Shang. Passing over Mount Yan, he met young Lei Zhenzi and was so impressed by the man's talent that he adopted him as his one hundredth son.

13. Wei Jiang with a pink three-tile face in *Orphan of the House of Zhao*, an opera adapted from an episode in *History of the Eastern Zhou*. Also called *Searching For and Saving the Orphan*, this is a story of murder and cruelty on the one hand and courage and sacrifice on the other. Tu Angu, a tyrannical general of the state of Jin, had ordered the execution of Zhao Shuo, son-in-law of Duke Ling of Jin, and his whole family. Only one member of this family, Zhao Shuo's baby son Zhao Wu, escaped death thanks to the help of Cheng Ying, a devoted friend of the Zhao family, who hid the baby in his house. Shortly afterwards the wicked general found out about this and ordered a ruthless search. Realizing that there would be great trouble if he did not give up the baby, Cheng Ying devised a plan: He had an infant child of his own that was about the same age as the Zhao family's orphan; since nobody outside his family had seen the two babies, perhaps he could hoodwink the general by giving up his own child, pretending it was the Zhao orphan. The trick worked and the sole survivor of the Zhao family was saved. Zhao Wu grew into a fine young man versed in both literature and the martial arts, and when the time came for him to enter the world, Cheng Ying told him the secret. True to the hopes of his savior and guardian, the young man avenged the murder of his family. Wei Jiang was a Jin general faithful to Zhao Wu. In the opera he personally kills the wicked Tu Angu.

14. Xian Mie with a black-cross steel-fork face in *Removing the Helmet Plume*, adapted from an episode in *History of the Eastern Zhou*. Xian Mie was a general of the state of Jin.

15. Ying Kaoshu with a red three-tile face in *Punishing Zidu*, adapted from an episode in *History of the Eastern Zhou*. Ying Kaoshu (?-712 B.C.) was a high official of the state of Zheng. When Duke Zhuang of Zheng made war on the neighboring state of Xu, Ying Kaoshu and Zidu, another Zheng general, both wanted to command the Zheng army. The command was given to Ying, who succeeded in taking the capital of Xu, but Zidu shot and killed him from behind during the battle, then returned to claim credit for the victory for himself. In the opera Ying Kaoshu's ghost appears during the victory banquet, forces Zidu to confess his guilt, and then strangles him.

16. Tu Angu with a flowered red-cross face in *Orphan of the House of Zhao*. Tu Angu, an official of the state of Jin, is the arch criminal in the opera.

17. Xu Jia with a white pointed three-tile face, the leading character in *The Silk Gown*, adapted from an episode in *History of the Eastern Zhou*. Xu Jia was a high official of Wei. In the opera he is sent on a mission to Qin, where he meets Fan Ju, Qin prime minister, whom he once vilified and who now pretends to be an impoverished person. He presents Fan with a silk gown and the latter, sensing that he still remembers their old relationship, chides and humiliates him but spares his life. Subsequently, the two become friends.

18. Ji Liao with an old yellow three-tile face, one of the leading characters in *The Dagger in the Fish*, adapted from an episode in *History of the Eastern Zhou*. Ji Liao was a king of Wu (r. 526-515 BC). A cruel and ambitious man, he dethroned his nephew, Ji Guang (King Helu, r. 514-496 BC), the rightful ruler. In the opera Ji Guang, to regain his throne, invites his uncle to a banquet and hires an assassin named Zhuan Zhu to murder him. The assassin, posing as a cook, serves fish with a dagger concealed in it. Setting the fish before the king, he pulls out the dagger and stabs the king to death.

19. Zhuan Zhu with a purple three-tile face, a leading character in *The Dagger in the Fish*. Zhuan Zhu was a soldier of Wu, brave, loyal, and upright. He helped Ji Guang kill his wicked uncle, Ji Liao, at a banquet, but was also killed himself during the scuffle.

20. Mi Nanwa with an inverted ingot face in *Wenzhao Pass*, adapted from an episode in *History of the Eastern Zhou*. King Ping of Chu, misled by the calumny of a wicked official called Fei Wuji, ordered Wu She, a high official, and his whole family to be executed. Only Wu She's son Wu Yuan managed to escape and he decided to flee to the neighboring state of Wu. On the way he had to cross Wenzhao Pass, which was guarded by Mi Nanwa. Fear of being caught turned his hair and whiskers white, but this concealed his identity, enabling him to slip through.

21. Li Gang with a flowered black-cross face in *A Picture of Qingyang*, adapted from an episode in *History of the Eastern Zhou*. Li Gang was a general under King Li of Zhou. When King Nan of Zhou was enthroned at Qingyang, he gave Li Gang the honorary title of Three Thousand Years (the honorary title of a king or emperor in feudal times was Ten Thousand Years).

22. Yi Li with a white eunuch's face in *The Golden Terrace*, adapted from an episode in *History of the Eastern Zhou*. Yi Li was a eunuch serving King Min (r. 300-284 BC) of Qi. King Min was an incompetent ruler who indulged in wine and women and neglected his court duties. Gradually Yi Li assumed control of all state affairs.

23. Lian Po with an old pink six-tenth face, a leading character in *Reconciliation of the General and the Minister*, adapted from an episode in *History of the Eastern Zhou*. Lian Po was a top general of the state of Zhao who, proud of his military achievements, refused to serve under Prime Minister Lin Xiangru, a younger man. Time and again, he tried to provoke the prime minister, but in the end was won over by the latter's patience and tolerance. To show repentance, he went to the prime minister's house, carrying a bundle of thistles on his back.

24. Hu Shang with a white flowered three-tile face in *Reconciliation of the General and the Minister*. King Zhao of Qin (r. 306-251 BC) sent him as an emissary to invite the king of Zhao to a meeting at Mianchi.

25. Jing Ke with a purple three-tile face, the leading character in *The Story of Jing Ke*, adapted from an episode in *History of the Eastern Zhou*. Jing Ke was a soldier of fortune of the last years of the Warring States period. He was hired by Dan (?-226 BC), crown prince of Yan, to assassinate the king of Qin, but failed in the attempt and was killed himself.

26. Wang Ling with a blue three-tile face in *The Gold Seal*, adapted from an episode in *Popular Romance of the Western Han*, a historical novel by Zhen Wei of the Ming dynasty. The novel begins with the kidnapping of Prince Yiren of Qin by the state of Zhao and ends with the death in 195 BC of Liu Bang, founder of the Western Han. Wang Ling, Liu Bang's friend, saved Liu Bang's family from his arch enemy Xiang Xu. After the Han dynasty was established, Wang was named Marquis of Anguo and served for a time as prime minister.

27. Zhao Gao with a watery white full face in *Sword of the Universe*, adapted from a story of the Qin Dynasty. Zhao Gao was a treacherous eunuch under Hu Hai, the second Qin emperor (r. 210-209 BC)

Hu Hai bestowed on Kuang Hong, one of his trusted ministers, a precious sword called the Sword of the Universe, with which Kuang Hong was permitted to execute any wicked person without reporting to the emperor first. Kang Jianye, a downright sycophant, ordered Zhou Que, his henchman, to steal the sword and present it to Zhao Gao, who had great power. Zhao Gao then ordered Zhou Que to disguise himself as a court attendant and assassinate the emperor. If the plot succeeded, he, Zhao Gao, would succeed to the throne. If it failed, he would accuse Kuang Hong of the assassination attempt. As things turned out, the plot failed, and Zhao Gao, after executing Zhou Que to head off a possible betrayal, presented the Sword of the Universe to the emperor, who became suspicious of Kuang Hong and clapped him in prison.

28. Xiahou Ying with an inverted ingot face in *Pursuing Han Xin,* adapted from an episode in *Popular Romance of the Western Han.* Xiahou Ying was a general under Liu Bang. He was ordered to set up an office to scout for talented people and persuade them to join Liu Bang's cause. Knowing that Han Xin was a very capable army commander, he recommended him to Xiao He, Liu Bang's chief counselor. Liu Bang, however, did not show much interest in the man, so one day Han Xin in great disappointment rode away. The opera tells how Xiao He and Xiahou Ying pursued him and won him back.

29. Ying Bu with a yellow broken-flower face in *Nine-Li Mountain,* adapted from an episode in *Popular Romance of the Western Han.* Ying Bu (?-195 BC) was originally Prince of Jiujiang, a general under Xiang Yu. He surrendered to Liu Bang, was named Prince of Huainan, and helped Liu Bang's commander, Han Xin, carry out the ambush on Nine-Li Mountain that trapped Xiang Yu at Gaixia. After the Han dynasty was established, he revolted against Liu Bang and was defeated and killed.

30. Peng Yue with a green broken-flower face in *Nine-Li Mountain.* Because he had distinguished himself in the ambush of Xiang Yu on Nine-Li Mountain, Liu Bang named him Prince of Liang after the founding of the Han dynasty. Later, however, he joined a revolt and was executed.

31. Xiang Yu with a black-cross and steel-fork face, the leading character in *The Prince Bids Farewell to His Favorite,* adapted from an episode in *Popular Romance of the Western Han.* During the wars between the Chu and Han, Xiang Yu (232-203 BC), Prince of Chu, was defeated by Liu Bang and trapped at Gaixia. In the opera the prince, hearing his enemies singing songs of Chu on all sides of Gaixia, realizes the game is up and bids a sad farewell to his beloved concubine, Yu Ji (?-202 BC). The latter, after performing a sword dance to comfort him, commits suicide. The prince then fights his way through the enemy and reaches the bank of the Wu River, but feels he can go no farther. Defeated and disgraced, he is too ashamed to return home, so instead of crossing the river he kills himself.

32. Lü Matong with a purple three-tile face in *Death on the River Wu,* adapted from an episode in *Popular Romance of the Western Han.* Lü Matong was formerly a general under Xiang Yu; later he surrendered to Liu Bang.

33. Yao Qi with an old black-cross face, the leading character in *Grass-Bridge Pass,* adapted from an episode in *Popular Romance of the Eastern Han,* a novel by Xie Zhao of the Ming dynasty. The novel begins with the establishment in AD 9 of Wang Mang's Xin dynasty and ends with the death in 167 of Emperor Huandi of the Eastern Han. Yao Qi was garrison commander of Grass-Bridge Pass. Because his son, Yao Gang, had killed

the emperor's grand tutor, he had his whole family, including himself, bound and taken before the emperor to be punished. It happened, however, that Ma Wu, another Han general, had just returned from the front to obtain recruits and he interceded with the emperor for Yao Qi and his family. Instead of punishing them, Emperor Guangwu sent Yao Qi and his son to the front to fight and atone for their crime.

34. Guo Rong with a watery white full face in *Grass-Bridge Pass*. The father of Emperor Guangwu's favorite concubine, he was killed by Yao Qi's son, Yao Gang.

35. Wu Han with a red three-tile face in *Capture of Luoyang*, adapted from an episode in *Popular Romance of the Eastern Han*. Wu Han (?-44) was the son-in-law of Wang Mang, founder of the short-lived Xin dynasty. He defected to Liu Xiu (later Emperor Guangwu of the Eastern Han) and, with Liu Xiu's generals Ma Wu and Cen Peng, stormed Luoyang and captured Su Xian, Wang Mang's garrison commander.

36. Wang Yuan with a red ingot face in *Capture of Luoyang*. An officer under Su Xian, he was killed when Luoyang fell to the armies of Eastern Han.

37. Niu Miao with a green broken-flower face in *Flying-Fork Formation*, adapted from an episode in *Popular Romance of the Eastern Han*. One of Wang Mang's top generals, he created the powerful flying fork battle formation that was invincible for a time. Ultimately, it was crushed by Ma Yuan, supreme commander of the Eastern Han armies.

38. Su Xian with an old pink six-tenth face in *Capture of Luoyang*. Ordered by Wang Mang to defend Luoyang, he was taken prisoner when the city fell to the armies of Eastern Han.

39. Yao Gang with a flowered black-cross face in *One-Sword Huang,* adapted from an episode in *Popular Romance of the Eastern Han*. One-Sword Huang was a tyrant of Huangtu Ridge. When Yao Gang, Yao Qi's son, was sent to the front for killing the emperor's tutor, he passed over this ridge and seeing the people there being mistreated, killed both the tyrant and his brother.

40. Ma Wu with a blue broken-flower face, a leading character in *Capture of Luoyang*. He was one of the twenty-eight generals of Yuntai who helped Emperor Guangwu found the Eastern Han dynasty. A very able general, he fought with distinction in the strategic battle for Luoyang.

41. Zhang Fei with a black-cross butterfly face, the leading character in "Reed Marsh," an act in the opera *Sweet-Dew Temple*. This opera is adapted from an episode in *Romance of the Three Kingdoms*, a long historical novel and literary classic by Luo Guanzhong (c. 1330-1400), a scholar of the late Yuan and early Ming. The novel is based on Chen Shou's *History of the Three Kingdoms,* Fan Ye's *History of the Later Han,* the Ming dynasty *Storyteller's Version of the History of the Three Kingdoms,* and various related legends and anecdotes. It is the story of the last years of the Eastern Han and the three kingdoms of Wei, Shu, and Wu, which lasted from 184 to 280. Focusing on the contradictions and struggles between rival feudal cliques, it creates vivid images of such famous historical figures as Liu Bei, Guan Yu, Zhang Fei, Zhuge Liang, Cao Cao, and Sun Quan.

Zhang Fei was a general of the kingdom of Shu. In the act "Reed Marsh" he is ordered by Zhuge Liang, prime minister of Shu, to disguise himself as a fisherman and hide in a marsh to wait for Liu Bei, who is returning to Jinzhou from Wu and is being pursued by Zhou Yu, the Wu commander-in-chief. He ambushes and captures Zhou Yu and then releases him, but Zhou Yu, incensed by his defeat and disgrace, vomits blood and dies.

42. Pang Tong with a purple Taoist face in *Laiyang County,* adapted from a story in *Romance of the Three Kingdoms.* When Pang Tong left Sun Quan to offer his services to Liu Bei, the ruler of Shu, the latter, unaware of the man's extraordinary ability, made him magistrate of Laiyang, a small county. For months Pang Tong neglected his magisterial duties, until one day Zhang Fei arrived at Laiyang on an inspection tour and chided him for his negligence. Pang Tong ordered his assistants to bring him all the work that had piled up. In less than half a day he went through the entire backlog of a hundred days and adjudicated each case carefully and correctly. The astonished Zhang Fei reported this to Liu Bei, who thereupon made Pang Tong deputy commander-in-chief of the armies of Shu.

43. Guan Yu with a red full face, the leading character in "Huarong Path," an act in the Peking opera *Battle of Red Cliff.* Cao Cao, the ruler of Wei, was totally defeated in the battle, and Zhuge Liang sent his generals to intercept him at various places along the route of his retreat. He assigned no task to Guan Yu (?-219) however, who was then Shu's top general. When Guan Yu remonstrated and demanded a part in the battle, Zhuge Liang ordered him to prepare an ambush at Huarong Path. Cao Cao arrived at the path with only eighteen followers and begged Guan Yu to let him pass. The old general, unable to forget how generously Cao Cao had once treated him, ordered his troops to disperse, allowing Cao Cao and his stragglers to slip through.

44. Zhou Cang with a tile-gray flowered ingot face in "Huarong Path." Zhou Cang was an officer under Guan Yu and a great warrior. At Huarong Path his thunderous shouts struck terror into the hearts of Cao Cao and his men.

45. Wei Yan with a flowered purple-cross face in *Battle of Changsha,* based on an episode in *Romance of the Three Kingdoms.* Wei Yan was a general of Changsha city. When Guan Yu was ordered byLiu Bei to attack the city, Han Xuan, prefect of Changsha, sent Huang Zhong out to fight him. Huang Zhong was over sixty but still a formidable swordsman; few were his match. Therefore, when he failed to vanquish Guan Yu after several battles, Han Xuan suspected him of treason and ordered his execution. Fortunately Wei Yan, returning with a convoy of grain, arrived on the scene and killed Han Xuan. He then surrendered Changsha to Guan Yu and, with Huang Zhong, joined Liu Bei's cause.

46. Yan Yan with an old pink six-tenth face in *Passing Through Bazhou.* Yan Yan was the garrison commander of Bazhou. When Zhang Fei arrived at Bazhou on his way to conquer western Sichuan, he was stopped by Yan Yan. The two fought several indecisive battles, but finally Zhang Fei managed to outwit Yan Yan and capture him. He treated his prisoner with great courtesy and Yan Yan not only surrendered but helped him take many other strategic passes on the way.

47. Meng Da with an inverted ingot face in *Retreat to Maicheng,* adapted from an episode in *Romance of the Three Kingdoms.* Meng Da was a general of Shu. Guan Yu, top general of Shu and so arrogant that he always underestimated his enemies, was badly defeated by the combined armies of Wu and Wei and forced to take refuge in Maicheng. He sent an emissary to Meng Da in a nearby city to ask for help, but Meng Da, who had an old grudge against Guan Yu, refused to help him. In desperation

Guan Yu tried to break through the enemy and was ambushed and killed.

48. Sha Moke with a red broken-flower face, a general of West Qiang nationality in *The Chain Camps*. He assisted Liu Bei of Shu in a war against Sun Quan of Wu. See 79 for the story of *The Chain Camps*.

49. Jiang Wei with a red three-tile face, the leading character in *Iron-Cage Mountain*, adapted from an episode in *Romance of the Three Kingdoms*. Jiang Wei was Zhuge Liang's disciple and commander of the armies of Shu after Zhuge Liang's death. In the opera he traps the Wei commander, Sima Shi, on Iron-Cage Mountain, but is defeated when Wei reinforcements arrive.

50. Zhang Bao with a flowered black-cross face in *The Junior Peach Garden Brotherhood,* an episode in *Romance of the Three Kingdoms*. To avenge the deaths of his sworn brothers Guan Yu and Zhang Fei, Liu Bei ordered an invasion of Wu. Guan Yu's son, Guan Xing, and Zhang Fei's son, Zhang Bao, both wanted to lead the vanguard and nearly came to blows. Liu Bei reminded them of the oath of brotherhood sworn by their fathers in a peach garden, whereupon the two young men also became sworn brothers and vowed to fight together to avenge the deaths of their fathers.

51. Xiahou De with a green broken-flower face in *Dingjun Mountain*, an episode in *Romance of the Three Kingdoms*. Xiahou De was commander of Cao Cao's army on Tiandong Mountain. He was killed by the old Shu general Huang Zhong in a battle at Dingjun Mountain.

52. Deng Ai with a white pointed three-tile face in *Tanshan Valley*, adapted from an episode in *Romance of the Three Kingdoms*. Deng Ai (197-264) was a high-ranking general of Wei. In the opera he is outwitted by Shu commander Jiang Wei and suffers a crushing defeat in Tanshan Valley.

53. Cao Cao with a watery white face, a leading character in *Meeting of the Elite*. In 208 Cao Cao (155-220) led a huge army to the Yangtze with the intention of crushing both Sun Quan and Liu Bei. Pang Tong, a military advisor of Sun Quan's at the time, tricked Cao Cao into chaining his ships together, saying they would move more steadily that way. Cao Cao was much pleased and held a sumptuous banquet on the river to celebrate his anticipated victory, during which he brandished a spear and composed a song to glorify his military successes. Shortly afterwards, Huang Gai, a general of Wu, pretending to surrender, sailed over to Cao Cao's camp and set fire to the chained ships. Cao Cao was completely defeated.

54. Xiahou Dun with a blue pointed three-tile face in *Bowang Slope,* adapted from an episode in *Romance of the Three Kingdoms*. One of Cao Cao's most trusted generals, Xiahou Dun was ordered to lead an army to take Xinye, but fell into an ambush laid by Zhuge Liang at Bowang Slope. The slope was set on fire, Xiahou's army was routed, and Xiahou himself barely escaped.

55. Dian Wei with a yellow flowered three-tile face in *Battle of Wancheng,* adapted from an episode in *Romance of the Three Kingdoms*. Dian Wei was a formidable warrior serving under Cao Cao. He used a pair of halberds, with which he vanquished all who opposed him. He played a decisive role in the Battle of Wancheng, forcing Zhang Xiu the defender of Wancheng city to surrender to Cao Cao. One day his enemies stole his halberds, then raided his camp at night and killed him.

56. Xiahou Yuan with a flowered black-cross face in *Dingjun Mountain,* adapted from an episode in *Romance of the Three Kingdoms*. The opera

shows how Zhuge Liang incited the old warrior Huang Zhong to fight Xiahou Yuan, one of Cao Cao's bravest generals and the defender of Dingjun Mountain. Huang Zhong takes Xiahou Yuan by surprise, kills him, and occupies the strategic mountain.

57. Xu Chu with a black broken-flower face in *Changban Slope,* adapted from an episode in *Romance of the Three Kingdoms.* This is the story of how Zhao Yun, a general of Shu, saved Liu Bei's baby son, Ah Dou. Carrying the baby against his chest, he fought off a succession of Cao Cao's toughest generals, including Xu Chu, at Changban slope and returned safely to Liu Bei's camp.

58. Zhang He with a crimson pointed three-tile face in *Changban Slope.* He was one of Cao Cao's best generals but could not stop Zhao Yun at Changban Slope.

59. Cao Hong with a red broken-flower face in *Changban Slope.* Although one of Cao Cao's bravest generals, he drew back when he met Zhao Yun on the battlefield and learned who he was.

60. Xu Huang with a white pointed three-tile face in *Retreat to Maicheng.* A general of Wei, he and Wu general Lü Meng attacked Guan Yu from two sides, defeated him, and forced him to retreat to Maicheng.

61. Meng Tan with a black broken-flower face in *Crossing the Five Passes,* adapted from an episode in *Romance of the Three Kindgoms.* Early in their careers, Liu Bei and his two sworn brothers Guan Yu and Zhang Fei were badly defeated by Cao Cao. Liu Bei and Zhang Fei managed to escape, but Guan Yu was trapped on a hill. An old friend of Guan Yu's urged him to surrender and Guan Yu said he would do so only on condition that Cao Cao release him as soon as he knew where Liu Bei was, to which Cao Cao agreed. Cao Cao

treated Guan Yu very well, hoping to win him over completely, but Guan Yu could not forget his former master and sworn brother. One day, learning by chance of the whereabouts of the latter, he set out to find him. On the way he had to cross five passes guarded by Cao Cao's men. Meng Tan was the commander at one of those passes. He was killed by Guan Yu when he tried to stop him.

62. Kong Xiu with a purple pointed three-tile face in *Crossing the Five Passes.* Kong Xiu was the commander at Dongling, another of the five passes Guan Yu had to cross.

63. Cai Yang with a white pointed old three-tile face in *Reunion at Gucheng.* One day after leaving Cao Cao, Guan Yu learnt that Zhang Fei, his other sworn brother, was at Gucheng. He went there to see him, but Zhang Fei, knowing that Guan Yu had served Cao Cao for a time, did not trust him. His suspicions increased when Cai Yang, a Wei general, arrived with an army, but Guan Yu vindicated himself by slaying Cai Yang.

64. Qin Qi with a black asymmetric broken-flower face in *Crossing the Five Passes.* Qin Qi was Cai Yang's nephew and one of the generals killed by Guan Yu at the five passes.

65. Sima Yi, supreme commander of the armies of Wei, with a watery white full face in *The Ruse of the Empty City.* During a war between the kingdoms of Shu and Wei, Ma Su, a Shu general, committed a serious blunder which forced him to give up an important pass, Jieting. This exposed the city of Xicheng where Zhuge Liang, the Shu commander-in-chief, had his headquarters. Xicheng was virtually defenseless as most of Zhuge Liang's forces had been deployed elsewhere, and Sima Yi was approaching at the head of a large army. In the desperate situation, Zhuge Liang ordered all the gates of the city to be opened as

if nothing was about to happen, while he himself, sitting on top of the city wall, calmly played a musical instrument. Sima Yi was bewildered when he arrived and saw this. Knowing that Zhuge Liang was a cautious man who never took risks, he suspected a trap and ordered a retreat.

66. Sima Shi with a flowered red-cross face in *Iron-Cage Mountain*. The eldest son of Sima Yi, he became supreme commander of the Wei armies after his father's death. In the opera he is defeated by the Shu general Jiang Wei and encircled on Iron-Cage Mountain where there is only one spring with a small trickle of water. When he offers up prayers and sacrifices to the spring, it begins to flow profusely, saving him and his men from dying of thirst. Subsequently, Mi Dang, king of the Western Qiang, an ethnic minority, arrives at the head of a large army to assist Jiang Wei, but Wei general Chen Tai, a friend of Mi Dang's, persuades him to change his alliance. Together they totally defeat Jiang Wei and force him to retreat from the mountain.

67. Jiang Gan with a civilian clown face in *Meeting of the Elite*. Jiang Gan was one of Cao Cao's staff officers and a former schoolmate of Zhou Yu, supreme commander of the armies of Wu. In the opera Cao Cao dispatches him to Wu to try to win over Zhou Yu. Jiang Gan not only fails in his mission but is tricked by the Wu commander, who forges a letter in the names of Cai Mao and Zhang Yun, Cao Cao's naval commanders. The letter says that the two are awaiting an opportunity to murder Cao Cao and surrender to Wu. Jiang Gan steals the letter and flees back to the Wei camp. Cao Cao, ever suspicious of others, is furious when he reads the letter and summarily orders the execution of his two commanders.

68. Guo Huai, a Wei general, with a black broken-flower face in *Iron-Cage Mountain*. When Jiang Wei retreated from the mountain (see 66), Guo Huai galloped hard in pursuit. The Shu commander had lost his spear and all his arrows, and had only a bow in his hand. But when Guo Huai let fly an arrow at him, he ducked and caught the arrow. Then at an opportune moment he shot it back at his pursuer and killed him.

69. Dong Zhuo with a watery white full face in *Fengyi Pavilion*. Dong Zhuo was the grand tutor of Xiandi, the last of the Eastern Han emperors, and was a terrible despot. To get rid of this man, Wang Yun, a minister, devised a plan called "the interlocking stratagem" to sow discord between Dong Zhuo and his adopted son Lü Bu, a formidable warrior. He betrothed his adopted daughter, beautiful Diao Chan, to Lü Bu, then gave her to Dong Zhuo, pretending to Lü Bu that Dong Zhuo had ordered him to do so. One day Lü Bu and Diao Chan met secretly at Fengyi Pavilion and Diao Chan pretended to be very unhappy. While Lü Bu was trying to comfort her, Dong Zhuo suddenly appeared and chased him away. Diao Chan then pretended she had been abused by Lü Bu. This incident caused a misunderstanding and eventually a complete break between the father and son. In the end, Lü Bu killed Dong Zhuo.

70. Jia Hua with an inverted ingot clown face in *Sweet-Dew Temple*. Jia Hua was a general of Wu. In the opera he is ordered by Sun Quan, the ruler of Wu, to lie in ambush at the Sweet-Dew Temple to assassinate Liu Bei. The plot is discovered and reported to Sun Quan's mother who, in a great rage, severely reprimands her son. Sun Quan pretends he knows nothing about it and questions Lü Fan, one of his counselors, who puts the blame on Jia Hua. Sun Quan's mother wants to execute

Jia Hua, but Liu Bei intercedes and saves his life.

71. Ma Su with an oily white three-tile face in *Loss of Jieting*. Ma Su was one of Zhuge Liang's trusted staff officers. When a powerful Wei army was on its way to attack the strategic pass of Jieting, Ma Su volunteered to defend the pass. Zhuge Liang cautioned him against belittling the enemy, but he vowed that nothing would go wrong and signed a pledge to be executed if he failed. Because of his arrogance and overconfidence in himself, he refused to take the advice of Wang Ping, his second in command, when they arrived at the pass. Instead of guarding the important approaches to the pass, he stationed his troops on a nearby mountain where they were quickly surrounded by the enemy. His blunder led to the loss of Jieting and forced Zhuge Liang's whole army to retreat. To enforce discipline, Zhuge Liang tearfully ordered the execution of his long-time friend and advisor.

72. Cheng Pu with a crimson three-tile face in *The Two Qiao Sisters of Phoenix Terrace*. In the last years of the Eastern Han, when the country was in great disorder, Qiao Xuan, an official, resigned his post and returned to Danyang, his hometown. With the intention of helping talented people restore order in the country, he established the Phoenix Terrace where he recruited a volunteer corps. Qiao had two beautiful daughters, who were very capable and ambitious. The elder daughter married Sun Ce (175-200), Sun Quan's elder brother and founder of the kingdom of Wu, and the younger daughter married Zhou Yu, supreme commander of the armies of Wu. Cheng Pu was a senior general of Wu who served under both Sun Ce and Sun Quan.

73. Huang Gai, a senior general of Wu, with a red six-tenth face in *Meeting of the Elite*. To deceive Cao Cao, Huang Gai and Zhou Yu devised a ruse that required Huang Gai to be tortured. It was acted out at the Meeting of the Elite. Zhou Yu, pretending to be provoked by a remark Huang Gai had made, ordered the old general to be flogged. And Huang Gai, pretending to be humiliated, wrote a secret letter to Cao Cao, offering to surrender. Cao Cao was taken in, whereupon Huang Gai sailed across the Yangtze with 20 ships laden with fuel and set fire to Cao Cao's fleet. This was the beginning of the historic Battle of Red Cliff, in which Huang Gai performed exceptional service for Wu.

74. Lü Meng with a blue pointed three-tile face in *Retreat to Maicheng*. While Guan Yu was attacking Fancheng, Lü Meng, commander of the armies of Wu, secretly led his men dressed as merchants across the Yangtze and captured Jingzhou. Guan Yu was forced to retreat to Maicheng and later was ambushed and killed.

75. Sun Quan with a watery white face in *Sweet-Dew Temple*. Because Liu Bei had occupied Jingzhou, which Sun Quan also wanted, and refused to give it to Wu, Sun Quan and Zhou Yu devised a plan to bring Liu Bei to Wu and hold him hostage until he gave up Jingzhou. The plan was to offer Sun Quan's sister, Sun Shangxiang, to Liu Bei in marriage. Liu Bei, acting according to a counterplan made by Zhuge Liang, approached Qiao Xuan, an elder statesman of Wu and Sun Ce's father-in-law, and asked him to help secure the agreement of Sun Quan's mother to the marriage. The old lady granted Liu Bei an audience in the Sweet-Dew Temple and was very favorably impressed with her prospective son-in-law. Thus the marriage conceived as a bait became a reality.

76. Taishi Ci, one of Wu's ablest generals, with a

green broken-flower face in *Meeting of the Elite*. When Jiang Gan crossed the Yangtze to see Zhou Yu, the latter gave a banquet for his friend. Aware of the purpose of Jiang Gan's visit, Zhou issued an order at the banquet that no one was to talk about the war; only topics of friendship were allowed. Taishi Ci, sword in hand, was given the task of enforcing this order. Since nearly all of the most important civilian officials and generals of Wu were present at the banquet, Zhou Yu called it a Meeting of the Elite.

77. Jiang Qing, a general of Wu, with a blue pointed three-tile face in *Sweet-Dew Temple*. After marrying Sun Quan's sister, Liu Bei and his wife returned to Jingzhou. Jiang Qing, on Zhou Yu's orders, tried to intercept them on the way and was severely reprimanded by Sun's sister.

78. Ling Tong with a purple three-tile face in *Raiding the Wei Camps with 100 Horsemen*. Ling Tong and Gan Ning were two generals of Wu who were enemies. When Cao Cao invaded Wu, both generals wanted to lead a counterattack. In the opera Sun Quan orders Ling Tong to attack first. He is unsuccessful and nearly killed, but Gan Ning despite their enmity saves him. That night Gan Ning with only 100 horsemen makes a daring raid on the Wei camps, causing such consternation that Cao Cao agrees to make peace.

79. Zhou Tai, a Wu general, with a white pointed three-tile face in *The Chain Camps*. Liu Bei's sworn brothers Guan Yu and Zhang Fei both died in wars against Sun Quan. To avenge their deaths, Liu Bei mustered a huge army intending to conquer Wu and put Sun Quan to death. With the help of soldiers from the Nan Man nationality of south China, who were experienced fighters, he defeated the Wu

armies again and again. Finally, Sun Quan appointed youthful Lu Xun as his commander. Lu Xun was a very shrewd general, but Liu Bei belittled him, thinking he was only a scholar. As it was the height of summer, Liu Bei ordered his men to camp in the thick of woods. A long chain of camps extending nearly 700 *li* was built, which was exactly what Lu Xun had hoped for. At a least expected moment, he ordered his men to set fire to the camps and completely destroyed Liu Bei's army. Zhou Tai and other Wu generals pursued Liu Bei until the faithful Zhao Yun arrived, repulsed them, and escorted Liu Bei to safety in Baidi city.

80. Zhou Chu with a red broken-flower face, a leading character in *Root Out the Three Evils*, adapted from *History of the Jin Dynasty: Biography of Zhou Chu*. Zhou Chu (?-297) was a warrior with unusual strength of the Western Jin dynasty. In his youth he used to bully people in his hometown, but later he changed his ways. In the opera, the prefect of Yixing, disguised as an old man, approaches Zhou Chu and satirizes him by telling him a story of three evils: a tiger, a flood dragon, and Zhou Chu himself. After hearing the story, Zhou Chu repents his wicked ways, kills a tiger and a flood dragon, and turns over a new leaf. Later, because he has served his country well, he is given the title General of Jiancheng.

81. Yuchi Baolin with a flowered black-cross face in *Bailiang Pass*, adapted from an episode in *Romance of Luo Tong's Expedition to the North*. Yuchi Baolin was the son of Yuchi Gong, a famous general of the early Tang. See 84 for opera story.

82. Shan Xiongxin with a blue broken-flower face in "Execution of Xiongxin," an act in the opera *Fettering the Five Dragons*, adapted from an episode in *Romance of the Tang Dynasty*. In

the last years of the Sui dynasty, feudal lords all over the country fought each other for power. Luo Cheng, a general under Li Shimin, son of Li Yuan founder of the Tang dynasty, disposed of five feudal lords called the Five Dragons. His exploits are depicted in *Fettering the Five Dragons*. Shan Xiongxin was a general under the Prince of Zheng, one of the Five Dragons. He was captured by the armies of Tang, refused to surrender, and was executed.

83. Cheng Yaojin with a green broken-flower face in *Jia Family Chamber,* adapted from a story in *Romance of the Tang Dynasty.* Cheng Yaojin, Shan Xiongxin, and a number of friends, went to the home of an old lady to offer congratulations on her birthday. While there, they performed a ceremony in a room called Jia Family Chamber that made them sworn brothers. Later when Cheng Yaojin was arrested for robbing imperial revenue, the others stormed the prison and rescued him.

84. Yuchi Gong with a black six-tenth face in *Bailiang Pass.* Yuchi Gong was a general of the early Tang. In the opera he leads a punitive expedition against Bailiang Pass and there meets with his long-lost son Yuchi Baoling, whom he recognized by the steel rod the young man used as weapon. Together the father and son capture the pass and kill a long-time enemy. Because of their chance meeting, the opera is also called *Reunion of Father and Son.*

85. Jin Jia with a yellow broken-flower face, one of the 36 sworn brothers brought together by Shan Xiongxin in *Jia Family Chamber.*

86. Li Yuanba with a black bird-like face in *Four Flat Mountains,* based on a story in *Romance of the Tang Dynasty.* Li Yuanba was a son of Li Yuan, first emperor of the Tang dynasty. He was a man of unusual strength and courage, and is generally regarded as one of the greatest

warriors of the Sui-Tang period. When Sui emperor Yangdi in his wars to unify the country was stopped by a strong enemy force at the Four Flat Mountains, he called on Li Yuanba for help.

87. Tong Huan with a red broken-flower face, one of the 36 sworn brothers in *Jia Family Chamber.*

88. Li Mi with a purple six-tenth face in *Duanmi Cave,* based on a story in *Romance of the Tang Dynasty.* Li Mi (582-618) was the chief of a band of outlaws at Wagang Stockade. When the stockade surrendered to the Tang, he surrendered too. Later he rebelled and was pursued by Tang emperor Li Shimin to Duanmi Cave where, refusing all demands for surrender, he was shot to death.

89. Yang Lin with an old pink six-tenth face in *Raid on Dengzhou,* based on a legend. Qin Qiong, an outlaw, has been arrested for robbery and taken to Dengzhou. His companions sneak into the city to rescue him. Yang Lin, a prince, learning of this devises a plan to annihilate the outlaws. His plan, however, is upset when a red lantern he hung up as a signal is shot down by the outlaws, who rescue Qin Qiong amid the turmoil.

90. Xin Wenli with a black broken-flower face in *Rainbow Pass,* a traditional opera of unknown origin. A band of outlaws attack the pass. Sui general Xin Wenli, the garrison commander, is shot to death by Wang Bodang, one of the outlaws. His wife Dongfang Shi, also a skilled warrior, assumes command and captures Wang Bodang. Instead of killing her prisoner to avenge the death of her husband, she falls in love with the handsome and courageous young man and sends her maid to persuade him to surrender and marry her. Wang Bodang pretends to agree, but on their wedding night he chides Dongfang Shi for her

unfaithfulness and kills her.

91. Qin Ying with a red bird-like face in *Golden Water Bridge,* a traditional opera of unknown origin. One day, when Qin Ying is fishing at the Golden Water Bridge, a local despot called Shan comes along and creates so much noise that the fish are frightened away. Instead of offering an apology, he chides Qin Ying for being in his way and the young man in a fit of anger strikes him with a rod, unintentionally killing him. Because the despot happens to be the emperor's father-in-law, Qin Ying's mother, Princess Yinping, trusses up her son and takes him to the palace to be punished. The emperor relents when the empress and their eldest grandson intercede on Qin Ying's behalf, and the case is settled with Princess Yinping making an apology and Qin Ying being sent to the front.

92. Dou Yihu with a green broken-flower face in *Chessboard Mountain,* based on the *Complete Story of the Western Expedition.* Xue Dingshan, a Tang general, and his mother and younger sister, Jinlian, are on their way to Suoyang Pass. While crossing Chessboard Mountain, they are captured by Dou Yihu, chief of the mountain stockade, and his sister Xiantong. Cheng Yaojin, one of Dou's companions, urges the stockade chief to free the captives and surrender to the Tang, but Dou insists on marrying Xue Dingshan's sister first. Cheng pretends to agree to this, but secretly arranges a marriage between Xue Dingshan and Dou's sister Xiantong.

93. Xue Gang with a black broken-flower face in *Jiuxi Palace,* adapted from the novel *Xue Gang Rebels Against the Tang.* Xue Gang was Xue Dingshan's son. In the opera the father and son have been slandered by two treacherous court officials, Zhang Tianzuo and Zhang Tianyou, and are about to be

punished. Cheng Yaojin, a prince living in Jiuxi Palace, goes to the emperor and exposes the two wicked officials. The emperor, realizing that he has made a mistake, pardons Xue Dingshan and his son.

94. Xue Kui with a black broken-flower face in *Xu Ce Rushes Around the City,* based on a story in *Xue Gang Rebels Against the Tang.* Xue Kui was Xue Gang's son. In the opera Xue Jiao, who is Xue Gang's nephew, is falsely accused of a crime by a wicked official called Zhang Tai. Carrying a letter from Xu Ce, a Tang minister and his adoptive father, he flees Chang'an to join his uncle and Xue Kui, and together they attack Chang'an. When Xu Ce hears of their attack he rushes to the top of the city wall to size up the situation, and then rushes into the imperial palace to ask that Xue Jiao's wrong be redressed. After the emperor executes the wicked Zhang Tai, Xu Ce persuades Xue Gang and Xue Kui to withdraw their forces.

95. Su Baotong with a black broken-flower face in *Jiepai Pass,* based on an episode in *Complete Story of the Western Expedition.* Tang emperor Taizong orders an expedition against the Western Regions. Qin Huaizhi is in supreme command, and Luo Tong, Duke of Yue, in command of the vanguard. When they arrive at Jiepai Pass, Su Baotong, garrison commander of the pass, wounds Qin Huaizhi with a dart. Luo Tong fights Su Baotong and wounds him with a blow from his whip, but in the end, his strength exhausted, he is killed by Su.

96. An Dianbao with a white pointed three-tile face in *One-Wood Pass,* based on an episode in *Complete Story of the Eastern Expedition.* An Dianbao was a general of minority nationality who guarded One-Wood Pass. A very able general, he defeated the Tang armies sent against him in many battles. In the opera he

inflicts a crushing defeat on Tang commander Zhang Shigui and captures his son and son-in-law. Zhang Shigui is a mean and selfish man who on many occasions has claimed credit for victories that rightly belonged to Xue Rengui, the greatest of the Tang generals. But now, in despair, he is forced to go to Xue for help. Although very sick, Xue rises from bed immediately he hears of the urgency, buckles on his armor, and rides to the pass. There, in a thrilling single-handed combat, he vanquishes the formidable An Dianbao.

97. Ba Lan with an old red three-tile face in *Princess Hundred Blossoms,* a new history play. Hundred Blossoms was a Kucha princess of the Tang dynasty. In the opera she is deceived by an enemy spy and, against the advice of veteran Ba Lan, leads an isolated force into battle. She is trapped and nearly captured by the enemy, but Ba Lan rescues her and kills the spy.

98. Yuwen Chengdu with a yellow flowered three-tile face in *Nanyang Pass,* based on a story in *Romance of the Tang Dynasty.* Yuwen Chengdu was a general under Yang Guang, later Emperor Yangdi of the Sui dynasty. He is revered as the second greatest warrior of the Sui-Tang period. In the opera Yang Guang kills a man called Wu Jianzhang and his family. The only survivor, a son called Yunzhao, happens to be the garrison commander of Nanyang Pass. Afraid that Yunzhao will revolt, Yang Guang sends troops to arrest him and bring him to the capital. Yuwen Chengdu is in command of a reserve force in the attack on Nanyang Pass. After being defeated in several battles, Yunzhao flees.

99. He Tianlong with a white pointed three-tile face in *Yandang Mountain,* a new history play based on stories of the Sui-Tang period. He Tianlong was the Sui emperor's garrison commander on Yandang Mountain. He fought a series of battles with rebel armies during the last years of the Sui.

100. Bao Zi'an with an old white three-tile face in *Reconciliation Between the Ba and Luo Families,* adapted from an episode in *Green Peony,* a novel of the Qing dynasty. *Reconciliation* tells about a young man, Luo Hongxun, on the way to his wedding in Shandong Province. When passing over Wild Jujube Ridge, he gets into trouble with Ba Jie, chief of the Ba Family Stockade, because he does not know their language. Ultimately, through the mediation of two greenwood heroes, Bao Zi'an and Fatty Huang, Luo's family is reconciled with the Ba family.

101. Fatty Huang with a yellow monk face in *Reconciliation Between the Ba and Luo Families.* Fatty Huang was a monk skilled in the martial arts.

102. Gai Suwen with a blue flowered three-tile face in *The Silted River,* adapted from an episode in *Complete Story of the Eastern Expedition.* Gai Suwen was a general of the state of Liao. In the opera Tang emperor Taizong runs into this Liao general while on a hunting trip. He tries to flee but the hooves of his horse sink into the silt of a nearby river. Gai Suwen catches up with him and demands that he sign a document of surrender. Luckily, Xue Rengui arrives and drives the Liao general away.

103. The Orangutan's Courage with a blue symbolic face in *Skyscraper Mountain,* adapted from an episode in *Complete Story of the Eastern Expedition.* The Orangutan's Courage was the nickname of the garrison commander of Skyscraper Mountain. Confident that the difficult terrain of the mountain was impassable, he neglected his defenses. Tang general Xue Rengui defeated him by a clever

ruse and captured the mountain.

104. Ba Jie with a black broken-flower face in *Reconciliation Between the Ba and Luo Families.* Ba Jie was the chief of the Ba Family Stockade on Wild Jujube Mountain.

105. Zhu Wen with a green flowered three-tile face in *Yaguan Tower,* adapted from a story in *Romance of the Late Tang and Five Dynasties,* a historical novel. The novel begins with the peasant uprising led by Huang Cao in 875 and ends with the revolt of Zhao Kuangyin and Chen Qiao that led to the establishment of the Northern Song. *Yaguan Tower* is about a bet between the Prince of Jin, Li Keyong, and Prince of Liang, Zhu Wen. The two princes are feasting in Yaguan Tower when a rebel army under Meng Juehai arrives. Li Keyong wagers that he can capture the rebel general before noon. Zhu Wen accepts the bet, using his jade belt as stake. But when Li Keyong's general, Li Cunxiao, returns with the captured rebel general, Zhu Wen refuses to honor his word. In a rage, Li Cunxiao seizes the belt from him. The incident causes a split between the two princes who until now have been allies.

106. Li Keyong with a red six-tenth face in *The State of Shatuo,* based on a story in *Romance of the Late Tang and Five Dynasties.* Li Keyong was the ruler of the state of Shatuo. In the last years of the Tang dynasty, when peasants led by Huang Chao rose in rebellion, the emperor of Tang conferred on Li Keyong the title of Prince of Jin and dispatched an emissary to Shatuo to enlist his aid.

107. Meng Juehai with a red broken-flower face, a leading character in *Yaguan Tower.* Meng was a general under Huang Chao, leader of a peasant uprising in the last years of the Tang dynasty.

108. Hu Li with a symbolic warrior-clown face in *Reconciliation Between the Ba and Luo Families.*

Hu was a shopkeeper who helped to effect the reconciliation. See 100.

109. Guo Ziyi with an old pink six-tenth face, a leading character in *Bed Full of Tablets,* adapted from an episode in the historical novel *Romance of the Sui and Tang Dynasties.* Because of his services to the Tang emperor during the An-Shi Rebellion, Guo Ziyi was made the Prince of Fenyang. On his 60th birthday, so many people came to offer their congratulations, each carrying a small tablet as was the custom in those days, that the prince's bed was loaded with tablets. Guo Ziyi's sixth son, Guo Ai, was married to the emperor's daughter, Princess Shengping. The princess, however, felt that she had married someone beneath her and treated her in-laws with great disrespect. All of Guo Ziyi's other sons and daughters came with their spouses to his birthday celebrations, but Princess Shengping deliberately stayed away and Guo Ai, standing alone among the couples, became an object of ridicule. Enraged and humiliated, he went home and gave his wife a beating. When the princess reported this to her parents, Guo Ziyi in haste took his son to the palace to be punished. The emperor, however, acted with reason and restraint. Instead of punishing Guo Ai, he promoted him and ordered his daughter to apologize to her in-laws. Thus a family feud was avoided and the husband and wife were reconciled.

110. Zhou Dewei with a red three-tile face in *Pearl Screen Stockade,* adopted from a story in *Romance of the Late Tang and Five Dynasties.* Zhou was the chief of Pearl Screen Stockade. A Tang army under Li Keyong arrived to take the stockade, and Zhou challenged the Tang commander to an archery duel. When Li Keyong shot down two vultures with one arrow, Zhou acknowledged defeat and sur-

rendered.

111. Wang Yanzhang with a green broken-flower symbolic face in *Fighting the Five Dragons,* adapted from a story in *Romance of the Late Tang and Five Dynasties.* Wang Yanzhang, a greenwood hero, is attacked by five fierce Tang generals known as the Five Dragons. He fights well but in the end, exhausted and unable to extricate himself, commits suicide.

112. Yu Hong with a black broken-flower face in *The Ruse of the Bamboo Grove,* adapted from a story in *Three Expeditions Against the Southern Tang.* Yu Hong was a Southern Tang general. In the opera he captures a Song general by witchcraft, but Liu Jinding, a woman warrior of the Song, sets fire to the bamboo grove in which he is hiding and forces him to flee.

113. Zheng Ziming with a black asymmetric flowered face in *Execution of the Yellow Robes,* based on an anecdote about Zhao Kuangyin, first emperor of the Northern Song. After the death of Emperor Shizong of the Later Zhou, Zhao Kuangyin, with the help of Generals Zheng Ziming and Gao Huaide, succeeded to the throne and established the Song dynasty. One day a man called Han Long came along and offered his sister to Zhao Kuangyin as a concubine. The emperor not only rewarded him with a title but gave him the privilege of parading through the streets to show off his honors. This so enraged Zheng Ziming that he went up to Han Long and slapped him in the face, whereupon the latter, conniving with his sister, brought a false charge against the general. Zhao Kuangyin, who was drunk at the time, ignored the protestation of Gao Huaide and had Zheng Ziming executed. Zheng's wife Tao Sanchun, hearing of this, led an army and encircled the capital. Meanwhile, the emperor, having recovered from his drunkenness, regretted his terrible mistake and beseeched Gao Huaide to mediate with the rebel army. Gao had Han Long executed first, then negotiated a settlement with Zheng's wife whereby she was allowed to cut in two the yellow robes Zhao Kuangyin wore as a token execution of the emperor.

114. Huyan Zan with a black broken-flower face, a leading character in *Dragon-Tiger Fight,* based on an episode in the novel *Romance of the Yang Family* which tells how several generations of the Yang family helped defend the Northern Song against invasions by the states of Liao and Xia. In the opera Huyan Zan's father is murdered by Song prime minister Ouyang Fang, and Huyan Zan leads an army to the capital to avenge his death. As none of the Song generals is his match, Zhao Kuangyin the emperor comes out in person to persuade him to surrender. Huyan Zan, not knowing who Zhao Kuangyin is, refuses and the two begin to fight. When Zhao strikes at Huyan with his golden rod, he sees the specter of a tiger shielding his adversary; and when Huyan lashes at Zhao with his steel whip, a phantom dragon appears. Knowing what the dragon symbolizes, Huyan realizes he is fighting the emperor and surrenders.

115. Zhao Kuangyin with a red full face in *Dragon-Tiger Fight.* Zhao Kuangyin, founding emperor of the Northern Song dynasty, reigned from 960-976.

116. Cui Zijian with a flowered purple-cross face in *The Gold Belt,* an opera of unknown origin that tells about the marriages of the sons and daughters of three families — the Cuis, Yangs, and Shes. In one of the acts, Yang Gun, a senior member of the Yang family, meets Zhao Kuangyin on the battlefield. He raises his battle-axe to strike Zhao, but at that instant Zhao turns into a dragon. Realizing that his adversary is the emperor, Yang surrenders.

Zhao confers on him the title of First Prince and presents him with the gold belt he is wearing.

117. Gao Wang with a black-cross face in *Herding Tigers Pass,* adapted from a story in *Romance of the Yang Family.* Gao Wang was a general of the Yang family who, disgusted with the corruptness of the Song court, fled to a faraway place, leaving his family behind. Years later he and his wife and son were reunited at Herding Tigers Pass.

118. Han Chang with a red broken-flower face in *Yang Paifeng,* based on a story of generals of the Yang family. Han Chang was a general of the state of Liao, and Yang Paifeng a servant girl tending fires in the Yang family's mansion. In the opera Han Chang captures Yang Zongbao, a general of the Yang family, and Yang Paifeng offers to go and rescue him. Although only a servant girl, she has practiced the maritial arts since childhood. She is laughed at for her foolhardiness, but to the amazement of all she overpowers Han Chang after a fierce hand-to-hand fight and brings Yang Zongbao back.

119. King Tianqing with a watery white full face in *Golden Sandbank,* adapted from an episode in *Romance of the Yang Family.* Tianqing was a ruler of the state of Liao. In the opera he invites Emperor Taizong of Song to a banquet at the Golden Sandbank, where he has set a trap to kill him. Song general Yang Jiye, aware of the plot, orders his eldest son, Yang Yanping, to go to the banquet disguised as the emperor and sends his other sons along as bodyguards. During the banquet Tianqing performs a sword dance, intending to stab Yang Yanping during the performance. But the latter sees through the trick and kills Tianqing with a weapon concealed in his sleeve.

120. Bai Tianzuo with a white flowered three-tile face in *The Relief of Hongzhou,* based on a story in *Romance of the Yang Family.* Yang Yanzhao, a general of the Yang family, is besieged by Liao general Bai Tianzuo at Hongzhou. A Song army commanded by the woman warrior Mu Guiying is sent to relieve the city. As the two rival armies face each other, Mu Guiying suddenly gives birth to a child. Despite the excruciating pain, she takes on Bai Tianzuo and defeats him.

121. Meng Liang with a red-cross gourd face in *Muke Stockade,* based on a story in *Romance of the Yang Family.* Meng Liang was a general of the Song army. In a war between the Song and Liao, the Liao army invented a battle formation called the Heavenly Gate. To smash this formation, the Song army needed weapons made of a special kind of wood grown in Muke Stockade commanded by Mu Guiying, a woman. Meng Liang and another man, Jiao Zan, were sent to the stockade to get the wood, by force if necessary. The opera tells about the intriguing events that took place before Mu Guiying finally agreed to give them the wood.

122. Yang Yande with a white monk face in *Wutai Mountain,* based on a story in *Romance of the Yang Family.* Yang Yanzhao, sixth son of the Yang family and supreme commander of the armies of the Northern Song, goes to the north to bring back the body of his father. On his way home, he stops at a temple on Wutai Mountain and there meets his long-lost brother Yang Yande. The two exchange a few questions before recognizing each other.

123. Jiao Zan with a black-cross face in *Muke Stockade.* Jiao was a Song general under Yang Yanzhao.

124. Yang Yansi with a black broken-flower face in *The Golden Sandbank.* Seventh son of the Yang

family, Yang Yansi and his brothers attend a banquet at the Golden Sandbank where the king of Liao has laid a trap to kill the Song emperor (see 119). The brothers fight their way out of the trap and return to the Song camp, but later Yang Yansi is murdered by a traitor.

125. Ba Ruoli with a black broken-flower face in *The Scholar Matchmaker,* a newly produced history play. Ba Ruoli, a Liao general, kidnaps Princess Chai of Song when she is hunting with the emperor along the country's border. Yang Yanzhao rescues her and later she marries him. Their matchmaker is a scholar called Lu Meng.

126. Pan Hong with a watery white full face in *Records of Upright Officials,* adapted from episodes in *Romance of the Yang Family.* Pan Hong, grand tutor of the Song emperor, has libeled and persecuted generals of the Yang family on many occasions. He is convicted and sentenced to death by Kou Zhun, an upright judge. During the trial, Pan's wife tries to bribe the judge but he declines all her gifts.

127. Fu Long with an old pink six-tenth face in *The Scholar Matchmaker.* A high official of the Song dynasty, he is punished for falsely claiming credit for the rescue of Princess Chai (see 125).

128. Tao Hong with an old warrior-clown face in *The Fight in a Melon Garden,* adapted from a legend of the Five Dynasties. Zheng En, an oil vendor, steals some melons from a garden owned by a man called Tao Hong. When caught, he refuses to admit his guilt and puts up a stiff fight. The garden owner is so impressed by his strength and courage that, instead of turning him over to the authorities, he marries him to his daughter.

129. Bao Zhen with a black full face, the leading character in *The Ungrateful Husband,* adapted from *Drumbeat Song of Qin Xianglian,* a folk tale. A drumbeat song is sung to the accompaniment of a drum. It used to be a popular form of entertainment in north China. The songs or stories were usually about struggles between honest and dishonest officials or wars against invasion. Al though they concerned mainly the doings of emperors, kings, ministers, and generals, they reflected to a greater or lesser degree the hopes of the common people and what they loved and hated. *Qin Xianglian* has been adapted into many kinds of operas. The Peking opera version is titled *The Ungrateful Husband.* It tells about the courage and selflessness of Bao Zhen(999-1062), a judge who defied the wrath of the imperial family and sentenced to death the emperor's son-in-law Chen Shimei. The latter, in order to marry the emperor's daughter, had not only disowned his legitimate wife and son but even tried to kill them.

130. Zhao Hu with a black broken-flower face, one of Judge Bao Zhen's bodyguards in *The Ungrateful Husband.*

131. Wang Chao with a purple three-tile face, one of Judge Bao Zhen's bodyguards in *The Ungrateful Husband.*

132. Ma Han with an ingot face, one of Judge Bao Zhen's bodyguards in *The Ungrateful Husband.*

133. Zhang Tianlong with a black symbolic face in *Double-Sand River,* adapted from a folk tale of the Song dynasty. Generals of the Yang family are sent to attack the state of Tubo. They are opposed by Zhang Tianlong, the Tubo king's son-in-law, and his wives Princesses Yubao and Yuzhen at the Double-Sand River. Enchanted by the handsome features of the Song generals Gao Neng and Yang Xian, the two princesses defect to them. Together they kill Zhang Tianlong.

134. Boy attendant with a clown face in *Theft of the Silver Flask,* adapted from a story in *The Book*

of *Thrillers, Second Impression.* This book was compiled by Ling Mengchu, a scholar of the Ming dynasty. It contains a collection of folk tales the author had picked up from time to time and rewritten in the form of a storyteller's scripts. *Theft of the Silver Flask* is also called *Fingered Citrons.* It tells about a Song empress who is taken ill and needs the fingered citrons grown in the state of Jin (Jurchen). An official called Zhou Bida is sent to buy them, but as Jin and Song are not on friendly terms, the official is detained by a Jin general. Later, Zhou Huiying and two other Song generals attack Jin. They rescue Zhou Bida and bring back the citrons.

135. Huyan Qing with a rubbed-in black broken-flower face in *Huyan Qing Takes Up the Challenge,* based on an episode in *Romance of the Huyan Family Generals with Golden Whips.* This is a story of the Song dynasty. Two great families, the Huyans and Ouyangs, were enemies because Ouyang Fang, Song prime minister and head of the Ouyang family, had executed a senior member of the Huyan family. Ouyang Fang's daughter was married to Pang Wen, a court official with great power whose own daughter was a royal concubine. In the opera Pang Wen and his daughter devise a heinous plot whereby the whole Huyan family is executed. Only Huyan Qing and his mother escape. One day news arrive from Youzhou that a man called Huang Wenbin is plotting to usurp the throne. To find good fighters, Pang Wen petitions to the emperor to let Ou Zifang, a monk skilled in the martial arts, set up a *leitai* (a stage on which challenge bouts are fought) and challenge all comers. Yang Wenguang, a general of the Yang family, comes along and gives Pang Wen a thrashing. Huyan Qing, out to avenge the murder of his family, also arrives. He

accepts the monk's challenge, goes on the stage, and after a furious bout beats his adversary to death. The enraged Pang Wen tries to arrest him, but with Yang Wenguang's help he escapes.

136. Wang Wen with a white pointed three-tile face in *Women Generals of the Yang Family,* a newly produced history play that tells how women generals of the Yang family, led by Dowager She and Mu Guiying, defeated Wang Wen, king of the Western Xia.

137. Han Zhang with a blue three-tile face in *The Three Chivalrous and Five Righteous,* an opera based on a novel with the same title. The first part of the novel tells how Han Zhang and four others, who were sworn brothers and knights errant, assisted a good judge Bao Zhen in righting the wrongs of the people and fighting corrupt officials. The second contains stories of how these knights errant themselves killed tyrants and saved innocent people. The themes of many Chinese operas are taken from this novel.

138. Xu Qing with a green broken-flower face, third of the five sworn brothers in *The Three Chivalrous and Five Righteous.*

139. Lu Fang with an old pink three-tile face, the eldest of the five sworn brothers in *The Three Chivalrous and Five Righteous.*

140. Jiang Ping with a warrior-clown face in *The Bronze Net Line,* adapted from an episode in *The Three Chivalrous and Five Righteous.* Zhao Jue, Prince of Xiangyang, plots to seize the throne of the Song dynasty. He builds for himself a castle protected by a line of fortifications called the Bronze Net Line. When Yan Chasan, an inspector-general, is sent by the emperor to Xiangyang, Zhao Jue steals his official seal and throws it into a pond within his fortifications. Bai Yutang, the inspector-general's bodyguard, tries to enter

the prince's castle to recover the seal and is killed in the attempt. Jiang Ping, a friend of Bai Yutang's, comes to Xiangyang and one night Bai's ghost appears before him in a dream and beseeches him to avenge his death. The next day Jiang Ping steals through the Bronze Net Line, dives into the pond, and recovers the seal.

141. Gongsun Sheng with a purple Taoist face in *Yellow Mud Ridge,* adapted from an episode in *Outlaws of the Marsh,* a long novel by Shi Nai'an of the late Yuan and early Ming. Centering on the peasant wars of the Song dynasty, the novel has created a host of popular heroes of Chinese fiction such as Li Kui the Black Whirlwind, Wu Song the Tiger Killer, Lin Chong a former captain of the imperial guards, and Lu Zhishen the Flower Monk, each of whom had a distinct character. Many Peking operas are adapted from episodes in this novel. *Yellow Mud Ridge* tells how the outlaws waylaid and seized a load of birthday gifts for the emperor's tutor. Gongson Sheng was one of the outlaws who took part in the robbery.

142. Liu Tang with a bottle gourd blue-cross face in *Xunyang Tower*. Song Jiang, while drinking in Xunyang Tower, takes up a brush and writes a rebellious poem on the wall. A spy reports this to the authorities, who arrest Song Jiang and sentence him to death. Liu Tang and other outlaws storm the execution ground and rescue Song Jiang, who is persuaded to join the outlaws on Mount Liangshan.

143. Chao Gai with an old yellow three-tile face in *Xunyang Tower*. Chao Gai was the chief of the outlaws of Liangshan in *Outlaws of the Marsh*. He led the raid on the execution ground that saved Song Jiang's life.

144. Lu Zhishen with a white monk face, the leading character in *Wild Boar Forest,* based on

an episode in *Outlaws of the Marsh*. Lin Chong, captain of the imperial guards, is convicted on a false charge and banished to Cangzhou. His guards have orders to murder him when they are passing through Wild Boar Forest, but Lu Zhishen, Lin Chong's sworn brother, follows them secretly, overpowers the guards, and saves Lin Chong.

145. Li Kui with a black broken-flower face, the leading character in *The Black Whirlwind*. Some bandits of Dingjia Mountain, posing as Song Jiang and Lu Zhishen, of Liangshan, kidnap a village girl. Li Kui, nicknamed the Black Whirlwind, who is unaware of the truth, knocks down the apricot banner of the Liangshan outlaws and curses their leader Song Jiang. Song Jiang offers to go down with him to the village to clear up the matter. After learning the truth, Li Kui goes to Song Jiang with a load of brambles on his back, a traditional way of begging forgiveness.

146. Yang Zhi with a blue broken-flower face in *The Birthday Gifts,* also called *Yellow Mud Ridge*. Liang Shijie, army commander at Damingfu, prepares a load of gifts for his father-in-law, the emperor's tutor, and orders Yang Zhi to escort the gifts to the capital. When the gifts are waylaid by Liangshan outlaws at Yellow Mud Ridge, and Yang Zhi goes away without asking leave, the commander, who has an old grudge against him, accuses him of being an accomplice. Eventually Yang is forced to join the outlaws.

147. Bai Sheng with a symbolic warrior-clown face in *The Birthday Gifts*. An outlaw of Liangshan, he poses as a wine dealer at Yellow Mud Ridge. When Yang Zhi arrives with the birthday gifts, he offers him and the other escorts wine mixed with sleeping powder. They drink it and fall asleep.

148. Wang Ying with a yellow flowered three-tile

face in *Cool Wind Mountain*. Wang Ying and Yan Shun are outlaw chiefs of Cool Wind Mountain. They capture Song Jiang but out of admiration for the man release him and treat him well. Later, when Song Jiang is in trouble, Wang Ying goes to his rescue.

149. Xuan Zan with a black broken-flower face in *Capture of Guan Sheng*. Guan Sheng was a general of the Song army. In the opera, he defeats the Liangshan outlaws in several battles, but eventually is captured by the outlaws and persuaded to join their cause. Xuan Zan is a subordinate of his.

150. Huyan Zhuo with a black broken-flower face in *The Chained Horses*. Huyan Zhuo, a Song general, is sent to attack the outlaws on Mount Liangshan. He defeats them with his formidable array of chained horses, but later a man called Xu Ning teaches the outlaws how to trip the horses with hook-spears. They annihilate Huyan Zhuo's army, capture the man, and persuade him to join their cause.

151. Qin Ming with a red broken-flower face in *Qingzhou Prefecture*. Formerly the garrison commander of this prefecture, Qin Ming is sent on an expedition against the outlaws on Cool Wind Mountain. He is taken prisoner and forced to join the outlaws.

152. Su Chao with a blue three-tile face in *Daming Prefecture*. He is the garrison commander of the prefecture. When Lu Junyi, an official of the prefecture, is jailed on a false charge, the outlaws of Liangshan decide to rescue him. Using a ruse devised by their counsellor Wu Yong, the outlaws enter Daming in disguise on the night of the Lantern Festival, surprise and capture Su Chao, and free Lu Junyi.

153. Zhou Tong with a black broken-flower face in *The Error of the Flower-Field Fair*. Liu Yuyan, a young lady, and her maid goes to a fair. There they meet a handsome and talented young man

named Bian Ji with whom the lady falls in love. When they return home, the maid tells the girl's father, Liu Deming, about it. Eager to find a good husband for his daughter, Liu sends a servant to the fair to invite the young man to his house, but through some misunderstanding the servant brings back the wrong person — a rascal called Zhou Tong.

154. Guan Sheng with a red three-tile face, the leading character in *Capture of Guan Sheng*. Sent by the Song government to attack the outlaws of Liangshan, Guan Sheng is tricked by Huyan Zhuo, one of the outlaws, who pretends to surrender to him. Huyan advises him to attack the outlaw stronghold at night. He does and is ambushed and captured.

155. Tang Long with a yellow broken-flower face in *The Wild-Goose-Plume Armor*. When the Liangshan outlaws are defeated by the Song army's chained-horse formation, Tang Long, one of the outlaws, tells their chief, Song Jiang, that the only way to smash the formation is to use a weapon called a hook-spear, and that his cousin Xu Ning can teach them how to use it. To get him to come to Liangshan, Tang Long sends a man to Xu Ning's house to steal his wild-goose-plume armor, a very valuable heirloom. When Xu Ning gives chase, he falls into a trap and is taken to Liangshan.

156. Yang Lin with a yellow flowered ingot face in *Shi Xiu Spies on the Village*. When the Liangshan outlaws are attacking Zhu Family Village, Song Jiang sends two spies, Yang Lin and Shi Xiu, into the village to gather information. Yang Lin, unfamiliar with the village lanes, is captured. But Shi Xiu, with the help of an old man, makes his escape and brings back information on the secret signals used by the villagers.

157. Zhu Long with a green broken-flower face in

Three Attacks on Zhu Family Village, an opera based on one of the most famous episodes in *Outlaws of the Marsh*. Zhu Chaofeng, the chief of Zhu Family Village, is a despot who, in collaboration with government soldiers, oppresses and terrorizes the local people. He also plans to attack the outlaws on Liangshan Mountain. One day he arrests Shi Qian, one of the outlaws, when the latter is passing through Zhu Family Village. The news infuriates the outlaws who, led by Song Jiang, attack the village. But Zhu Family Village is a well fortified place with high walls and a deep moat. In their first attack the outlaws, unfamiliar with local conditions, are repulsed and Song Jiang is nearly trapped. Drawing lessons from their initial defeat, the outlaws proceed more warily. By a clever ruse, they sow discord between Zhu Family Village and two other villages that are its allies, thus isolating their enemy. Next they send some of their men, disguised as villagers, into Zhu Family Village to work as inside agents. In this way, after a second and a third attack they take the village and kill the village chief and his sons and henchmen. Zhu Long is the chief's eldest son. He is killed by the outlaws during their attacks.

158. Zhu Hu with a blue broken-flower face in *Three Attacks on Zhu Family Village*. The second son of the village chief, he is killed by the outlaws when they take the village.

159. Luan Tingyu with a purple pointed three-tile face in *Three Attacks on Zhu Family Village*. A martial arts instructor, Luan Tingyu taught the villagers how to use the iron staff. When the village falls, he escapes.

160. Zhu Biao with a white twisted flowered face in *Three Attacks on Zhu Family Village*. The village chief's third son, he is also killed when the outlaws take the village.

161. Zhang Shun with a white flowered three-tile face, a leading character in *The Fight at Jiangzhou*. Song Jiang is banished to Jiangzhou for killing a man. One day when he and his friends Li Kui and Dai Zong are drinking at a tavern, Li Kui goes to buy some fish and gets into a brawl with Zhang Shun the fishmonger. Song Jiang comes and stops the fight, but not until Li Kui has been thrown into a pond.

162. Xu Shiying with a dark green broken-flower face in *Yanyang Chamber*, a traditional opera. Gao Deng, relying on the power of his father Gao Qiu, a eunuch of the Northern Song, tyrannizes the people of Nanyang. One day he abducts a local girl and keeps her in a room in his house called the Yanyang Chamber. The girl's elder brother Xu Shiying, with the help of four outlaws of Liangshan, enters Gao Deng's house at night, frees his sister, and kills the tyrant.

163. Ni Rong with a green broken-flower face in *The Qingding Pearl*, also called *The Fisherman's Revenge*. Xiao En and his daughter Guiying earn their living by fishing. One day Landlord Ding, a local tyrant, sends a henchman to demand payment of a fishing tax. Ni Rong and Li Jun, two friends of the fisherman who are drinking with him, chide the tax collector and force him to leave. The landlord now sends the captain of his guards and some hoodlums to extort the money, but they too are driven off by the fisherman and his friends. Fearing reprisal by the local authorities, the fisherman goes to the county court and reports the case. The county magistrate, however, is in league with the landlord. Instead of punishing the latter, he accuses the fisherman of disrupting the law and gives him a flogging. Sensing that there is no other recourse, the fisherman and his daughter go to the landlord's house to take revenge. Pretending that they have come to

present the landlord with a valuable pearl called Qingding, they enter the house and kill the landlord and his captain.

164. Shi Qian with a warrior-clown face, the leading character in *The Wild-Goose-Plume Armor.* Shi Qian is one of the outlaws of Liangshan. A man of great agility who can scale walls and climb roofs with ease, he is chosen by Wu Yong, the outlaws' military advisor, to go to the Eastern Capital of Song to steal the wild-goose-plume armor. See 155 for story.

165. Gao Deng with an oily white pointed three-tile face in *Yanyang Chamber.* See 162.

166. Dong Chao with a clown face in *Wild Boar Forest,* one of the two guards ordered to murder Lin Chong in the forest. See 144.

167. Gao Qiu with a watery white full face in *Wild Boar Forest.* A powerful eunuch and high official, he connives with his son in abducting the wife of Lin Chong and then falsely accuses Lin Chong of attempting an assassination and banishes him to Cangzhou. See 144.

168. Xue Ba with an ugly clown face in *Wild Boar Forest,* one of the two guards ordered to murder Lin Chong. See 144.

169. Hamichi with a warrior-clown face in *Lu'anzhou,* an opera based on a story in *Complete Biography of Yue Fei* by Qian Cai of the Qing dynasty. The biography centers on the wars waged by Yue Fei (1103-1142) and his generals against the Jin (Jurchen) which had invaded the Song empire. It paints a glorious picture of a brave, loyal, and patriotic general whose tragic death at the hands of traitors has been mourned by people down the centuries. Hamichi was a staff officer with the Jin army that attacked Lu'anzhou.

170. Jin Chanzi with a black-and-gold broken-flower face in *Striking Down the Golden Cicada.* Jin Chanzi, whose name is literally translated as "Golden Cicada," was a formidable general of the Jin (Jurchen) army. In the opera he wins a series of victories against the Song armies under Yue Fei. Hoping to take the edge off the enemy's fighting spirit by a stalemate, Yue Fei puts up signs refusing to fight any more battles. His son, Yue Yun, misunderstands his father's strategy and, accusing the Song generals of cowardice, smashes all the signs. His father orders him to fight the enemy to atone for his disobedience. To his great surprise, the young man kills the Golden Cicada with his powerful sledgehammer.

171. Chai Gui with a white pointed three-tile face in *Seeking Capable Men.* To find capable men to serve him, the Song emperor sponsors a tournament. Chai Gui, relying on his power as Prince of Liang and conniving with one of the judges, is determined to win first place by all means, fair or foul. On the day of the tournament, learning that he is slated to meet Yue Fei, he tries to coerce Yue Fei into backing out. Yue Fei not only refuses but challenges Chai Gui to a fight to the death. In the ensuing combat, he pierces Chai Gui with his spear and kills him.

172. Hei Fengli with a rubbed-in black hero's face in *Overturning the Battle Wagons,* an opera about Yue Fei's fight against the Jurchen general Wu Zhu at Niutou Mountain. Yue Fei's army is hardpressed in the early part of the battle. Gao Chong, one of his subordinates who has been ordered to guard the rear, comes up to help him and they rout the Jurchen army. Wu Zhu, the Jurchen commander, now orders Hei Fengli, one of his captains, to hurl his iron battle wagons down the mountain slope to block Yue Fei's advance. Gao Chong overturns a number of wagons, but in the end both he and his horse are exhausted and he is knocked down and killed.

173. Niu Gao with a flowered black-cross face in *The Dream of a Flying Tiger,* also called *Niu Gao Takes a Wife.* Niu Gao was a very able general under Yue Fei. In the opera he is sent to relieve Ouyang Pass which is besieged by a powerful Jurchen army. After he routs the besiegers, the garrison commander of the pass offers him his sister-in-law as wife. This woman is also an expert in the martial arts, so on their wedding night the husband and wife engage in a friendly duel in their bedchamber.

174. He Yuanqing with a red flowered three-tile face in *Qiwu Mountain.* Originally the garrison commander of Qiwu Mountain, He Yuanqing rebels against the Song. Yue Fei defeats and captures the rebel general in several battles, but each time he treats his prisoner leniently and lets him go. In the end, overwhelmed by the Song commander's generosity, He Yuanqing repents and surrenders, reaffirming his loyalty to the Song cause.

175. Di Lei with a black broken-flower face in *The Eight Sledgehammers.* The opera takes its title from the weapons used by four generals of the Song army, each of whom wielded a pair of sledgehammers. Di Lei was one of the four. The plot is based on an invasion of the Central Plains, the heartland of the Song empire, by a Jurchen army under Wu Zhu and his adopted son Lu Wenlong. Yue Fei, the Song commander-in-chief, orders his four sledgehammer generals to fight Lu Wenlong, but the formidable Jurchen general defeats every one of them. Wang Zuo, a prince of the Song, finds out something about Lu Wenlong's past. He is actually the son of a famous Song general who committed suicide after losing a battle to the Jurchens. His son was captured by the Jurchens, and Wu Zhu, the Jurchen commander, became his adoptive father. Wang Zuo now pretends to surrender to Wu

Zhu, cutting off his left arm as a token of his sincerity. Once in the Jurchen camp, he poses as a storyteller and through his stories reveals to Lu Wenlong how his father has faithfully served and died for his country. During a subsequent raid by the Jurchens on the Song camp, Lu Wenlong defects and helps Yue Fei defeat the attackers. He then joins Yue Fei.

176. Wu Zhu, or Jin Wu Zhu (?-1148), with a black-and-gold broken-flower face in *Niutou Mountain,* also called *Overturning the Battle Wagons.* See 172.

177. Li Tingzhi with a red ingot face in *Song of Righteousness.* Li Tingzhi was a general of the Southern Song dynasty and a friend of Wen Tianxiang. On his recommendation Wen Tianxiang was made the emperor's *right* prime minister, in charge of all military affairs. When Yuan emperor Kublai Khan invaded the Southern Song, Wen Tianxiang was sent over to the enemy to negotiate a peace. The Yuan commander detained him and urged him to surrender, but he refused. He remained in captivity for three years, during which he steadfastly rejected all demands for him to change his allegiance and in the end died a hero's death. Meanwhile, Li Tingzhi led an army to Yangzhou to defend the city against the Yuan invaders. He, too, ultimately gave his life for his country. By this time the Southern Song was already a lost cause.

178. Gold-eyed Monk with a purple monk face in *Two-Dragon Mountain,* adapted from a story in *Outlaws of the Marsh.* Gold-eyed Monk, Silver-eyed Monk, and Little Monk are asked by an official of Song to assist them in fighting the Liangshan outlaws. Arriving at Two-Dragon Mountain in the night, the three put up at an inn owned by Zhang Qing and his wife Sun Erniang. Zhang Qing is actually an outlaw of Liangshan in disguise. During the night he

and his wife murder the two elder monks, but Little Monk escapes.

179. Bo Yan with a tile-gray flowered three-tile face in *Song of Righteousness.* Bo Yan was the overall commander of the Yuan armies that invaded Southern Song.

180. Silver-eyed Monk with a blue monk face. In the opera *Two-Dragon Mountain,* he and Gold-eyed Monk are murdered by the Liangshan outlaw Zhang Qing and his wife. See 178..

181. Mu Ying with a yellow broken-flower face in *The Capture of Jinling,* based on a story in *The Lives of Heroes and Martyrs,* a Ming dynasty historical novel that begins with the downfall of the incompetent Yuan emperor Shundi in 1328 and ends with the establishment of the Ming dynasty by Zhu Yuanzhang. The opera tells how Zhu Yuanzhang attacked and captured Jinling (now Nanjing). Mu Ying was one of his generals.

182. Xu Yanzhao with a purple six tenths face, one of the central characters in *Second Entry into the Palace,* a traditional opera based on a drum ballad. When Ming emperor Muzong (r. 1567-1572) died, the crown prince was still an infant and Li Yanfei, the empress dowager, ruled behind the scenes. The dowager's father, Li Liang, plotting to usurp the throne, seals off the courtyard where his daughter is living so that she can get no news from outside. But two loyal ministers, Xu Yanzhao and Yang Bo, force their way into the palace twice to warn the empress of the situation. After their second entry the empress realizes that she has been deceived by her father. Moved by their loyalty, she entrusts to them the management of state affairs and commends her infant son to their care. Later Li Liang is executed by Yang Bo.

183. Jiang Zhong with a black flowered ingot face in *Bailiang Tower,* adapted from a story in *The Lives of Heroes and Martyrs.* A junior officer under Zhu Yuanlong, Prince of Western Wu, accidentally injures the uncle and younger brother of Liu Futong, Prince of Yingzhou. Liu vows to take revenge on Zhu. He builds a tower called Bailiang on Broken-Stone Mountain and conceals a store of gunpowder in it. Then he calls on various feudal lords to come to the mountain with their armies to discuss how to get rid of Zhu Yuanlong. Zhu, who has got wind of the plot, goes to the mountain in disguise, taking with him his two trusted generals Wu Zhen and Jiang Zhong. A fire suddenly breaks out. Zhu manages to escape, but Jiang Zhong, after fighting furiously, falls into a pit and is killed.

184. Chi Fushou with a red pointed three-tile face in *Capture of Jinling.* Chi was the son-in-law of the Yuan emperor. He defended Jinling against attacks by armies of the Ming. When overpowered by superior forces, he committed suicide.

185. Wanyan Long with a red broken-flower face in *A String of Dragon Pearls,* based on a story of the late Yuan dynasty. Wanyan Long was the Prince of Lu, a feudal lord and a monster who plundered and pillaged the people. According to the story, he and his henchmen used to go hunting, and each time they would trample over and destroy large tracts of good farmland. Once when a village head tried to reason with him, he had the man flogged and shackled as a lesson for the masses. At the suggestion of his wicked caretaker, he robbed a man of a precious string of dragon pearls and accused the owner of having stolen it. He murdered women and children at will, and once just to amuse himself hacked off a woman's left hand. Finally, Xu Da the magistrate of Xuzhou, unable to put up with such wickedness, revolted, killed the tyrant,

and fled to Haozhou to join Zhu Yuanzhang, who later founded the Ming dynasty.

186. Lou Ashu, or Lou the Rat, with a symbolic wicked-clown face, one of the central characters in *Fifteen Strings of Cash,* an opera based on a story in *Common Sayings to Alert the World. Common Sayings* is a collection of stories by Feng Menglong (1574-1646), a scholar and playwright of the late Ming who also wrote *General Sayings to Warn the World* and *Wise Sayings to Instruct the World.* The stories in them are written like the scripts used by storytellers in the old days. It is a style called *huaben* (story copy) first used in the Tang dynasty when people told or sang stories from the Buddhist scriptures. It developed and acquired a definite form during the Northern and Southern Song dynasties and became very popular during the Ming. A wide range of subjects is covered by the stories: love, oppression, struggle, friendship, perfidy, daily life. *Fifteen String of Cash* tells about a good-for-nothing gambler, Lou Ashu. He robs a butcher of 15 strings of cash, murders his victim, and tries to put the blame on the butcher's adopted daughter and a passer-by Xiong Youlan. The magistrate of Wuxi sentences the daughter and passer-by to death, but Prefect Kuang Zhong suspects something is wrong. He reexamines the case, finds out the truth, and brings the Rat to justice.

187. Yan Peiwei with a red ingot face in *Five Righteous Men,* adapted from *Records of the Loyal and Righteous* by Li Yu and others of the Qing dynasty. *Records* is the story of the struggle of the Eastwood Party and the people of Suzhou against Wei Zhongxian, a treacherous eunuch who held great power in the Ming court. The Eastwood Party was established in the late Ming by scholar officials who advocated reforms. Mao Yilu, Wei Zhongxian's adopted son, was governor of Suzhou at the time. In the opera he levies taxes and conscripts labor to build a temple in honor of his adoptive father. When the temple is completed, Zhou Shunchang, an honest and upright official, goes in and condemns the wicked eunuch in front of his statue. Hearing of this, Wei forges an imperial decree and has Zhou arrested and sent to the capital. The people of Suzhou, outraged by the injustice, stage an uprising led by Yan Peiwei and four others — the Five Righteous Men. They kill an officer, give Mao Yilu a beating, and pull down the temple.

188. Mother of Hua Yun with a female blue broken-flower face in *A String of Dragon Pearls.* She and her son Hua Yun joined the revolt led by Xu Da, the prefect of Xuzhou, against Wanyan Long and his father. See 185.

189. Li Qi with an asymmetric black broken-flower face in *The Trial of Li Qi,* an opera based on a story of the Ming dynasty. Li Qi, a bandit, is captured while trying to rob a high official's house. At his trial, he implicates a man called Wang Liang, against whom he has a grudge. Wang Liang is put in jail, but his servant Chen Tang, knowing of the deep love between Wang Liang and his wife, seeks out the bandit and begs him to clear his master. Moved by the servant's pleas, Li Qi revokes his original testimony and Wang Liang is acquitted.

190. Jia Gui with a comical eunuch face in *Famen Temple,* an opera based on a popular story of the Ming dynasty. Liu Jin, the chief eunuch in the imperial palace, accompanies the empress dowager to the Famen Temple to burn incense. While there, he is approached by a girl called Song Qiaojiao, who begs him to help clear a man wrongly accused of murder. Liu Jin gives the local magistrate three days to solve the case. During this time the real

murderer is apprehended and the wrongly accused person is freed. Jia Gui is an attendant of Liu Jin's. The opera exposes his servility in the presence of his superior and his arrogance towards the ordinary people.

191. Liu Biao with a slanting ingot face in *Famen Temple*. Liu Biao is the son of a matchmaker who has been asked by a girl called Sun Yujiao to arrange a marriage between her and Fu Peng, a captain of the imperial guards. On his way home one night, Liu Biao passes Sun Yujiao's house and finds that the door is only half closed. He enters, intending to take advantage of the girl in her sleep. The girl's maternal uncle and aunt are also in the house and are sleeping together. The intruder mistakes them for Fu Peng and Sun Yujiao having an affair. Already jealous of Fu Peng, he stabs the man, cuts off his head, and throws it into the backyard of Liu Gongdao, his own uncle. Song Xing'er, a hired worker, finds the head and hurriedly tells Liu Gongdao. Liu, frightened out of his wits, throws the head into a dry well and then, fearing that the worker will let out the secret, pushes him into the well too. The next morning Sun Yujiao's mother reports the case to the authorities. Fu Peng is arrested and under torture confesses to the false charges against him. Eventually the truth is brought to light and Liu Biao is arrested and executed. This murder and the one mentioned in 190 are parts of the same opera.

192. Liu Jin with a red eunuch face, the leading character in *Famen Temple*. Liu Jin was a eunuch in charge of court rituals during the reign of Ming emperor Wuzong. See 190.

193. Liu Lujing with a civilian clown face, the leading character in *A Visit to the Grave,* a traditional opera. Liu Lujing, a scholar of Shandong Province, has gone to the capital to take part in the imperial exams. He is away for so long that his wife thinks he is dead. On the Qingming Festival one year, she goes to their family graveyard to make offerings to her "dead" husband. At that very moment he reappears. He has not died; he has passed the exams with honors, been given a government post, and is now home to worship at his ancestral graves. Seeing a woman weeping at a grave who looks like his wife, he goes up to her and examines her closely but dare not recognize her. After questioning her carefully, he is at last convinced that she is indeed his own wife. Overjoyed, the woman takes off her mourning clothes and accompanies her husband to his new post.

194. Shen Yanlin with an ugly civilian-clown face in *Yutang Chun,* adapted from a story in *General Sayings to Warn the World.* Yutang Chun (literally "Hall of Jade in Spring") was a prostitute. Her real name was Zheng Lichun. After she was sold into a brothel, she changed her name to Yutang Chun. She also used the name Su San. In the opera she is resold by her procuress for a large sum of money to a rich merchant of Shanxi Province called Shen Yanlin. More troubles await her in her new home. The merchant's wife, Pishi, jealous of the young girl, tries to kill her, but one day a bowl of poisoned noodles she has prepared for her is mistakenly eaten by Shen Yanlin, who dies. The wicked Pishi now accuses Yutang Chun of poisoning her husband and the innocent girl is · thrown into prison. Eventually the case is solved, though not without great ordeals for Yutang Chun, and Pishi pays the death penalty for her crime.

195. Ben Wu with a clown-monk face in *Longing for the Secular,* adapted from the *Only Extant Copy of the Poetic Dramas of Yuan and Ming.* A young girl has lived in a convent on a mountain since

childhood. One day, no longer able to bear the loneliness of a nun's life, she runs away. On her way down the mountain, she meets a young monk called Ben Wu who has also renounced his monkhood. They fall in love and return to the secular world together.

196. De Lu with a young clown face in the *Imperial Monument Pavilion,* an opera adapted from a story called *On a Rainy Night.* Wang Youdao, a scholar, is away from home taking the imperial exams. His wife, at the request of her younger brother De Lu, returns to her parents for a visit. On the way she is caught in a rain and seeks shelter in a wayside pavilion called the Imperial Monument. A scholar called Liu Shengchun is also sheltering himself there. The two stay there the whole night, but neither says a word to the other, and in the morning when the rain has stopped they go their respective ways. Wang Youdao, however, is furious when he returns home and hears of this. Refusing to believe his wife, he divorces her. Later, convinced of the truth, he apologizes to his wife and they are reunited. Moreover, out of admiration for the scholar Liu Shengchun, he marries his younger sister to him.

197. Liu Zongmin with a red three-tile face in *The Banner of the Daring Prince,* a new history opera that tells how Li Zicheng, nicknamed the Daring Prince, and other leaders of peasant uprisings in the last years of the Ming dynasty quelled disturbances in the country and defeated the armies of Ming. Liu Zongmin was one of Li Zicheng's generals.

198. Chong Gongdao with an old clown face, a leading character in *Escorting the Woman Prisoner,* adapted from a story in *General Sayings to Warn the World.* Chong Gongdao, an old prison guard and a kindhearted man, is given the task of escorting a woman prisoner to Taiyuan to be retried. Learning of the prisoner's bitter experiences, he does his best to console her on the way. Eventually he adopts her as his daughter. This opera is actually an act in the opera *Yutang Chun* (see 195), and the prisoner is the prostitute Yutang Chun, wrongly accused of murder. The court in Taiyuan absolves her of the crime.

199. Hao Yaoqi with a rubbed-in red full face, one of Li Zicheng's generals in *The Banner of the Daring Prince.* See 197.

200. Xia with a red ingot face, a junior officer known only by his surname "Xia" in *White Water Beach,* adapted from *The Legend of the Tongtianxi Sword.* Xu Qiying, a chivalrous outlaw, comes down from his mountain stronghold. After drinking, he falls asleep on a stone slab and is discovered and arrested by some soldiers. Commander Liu Ziming orders an armed party headed by his son to escort the prisoner to the capital. When they are passing White Water Beach, Xu Qiying's sister and a number of outlaws ambush the guards, disperse them, and rescue the prisoner.

201. He Tianlong with a purple pointed three-tile face in *Chain-Bend Stockade.* The opera is adapted from an episode in a novel of the late Ming called *Magistrate Shi's Casebook,* which describes cases handled by Shi Shilun, magistrate of Yangzhou during the reign of Emperor Kangxi (r. 1662-1722). The novel contains much that is fictitious, designed to promote feudal ideas of chivalry and loyalty to emperor. *Chain-Bend Stockade* tells how an official of the Qing government disguised as an armed guard goes outside the Great Wall to visit Dou Erdun, chief of the stockade and a greenwood hero, and tricks him into admitting that he stole the emperor's horse. He Tianlong is one of Dou Erdun's followers.

202. He Tianbiao, another of Dou Erdun's

followers, with a green broken-flower face, a character in *Chain-Bend Stockade*.

203. Dou Erdun with a blue flowered three-tile face, the leading character in *Stealing the Imperial Steed*, based on a story in *Magistrate Shi's Casebook*. Liang Jiugong, representing Emperor Kangxi, goes hunting outside the Great Wall. He rides an imperial steed that can travel 1,000 *li* a day. Outlaws of Chain-Bend Stockade hear about this and report to their chief, Dou Erdun. The latter has a grudge against Huang Santai, an officer under Liang Jiugong, and is determined to get even with him. He goes secretly into Liang's camp at night, kills a night watchman, and steals the horse, then leaves behind a poem implicating Huang Santai. As Huang Santai is already dead, the authorities order his son, Huang Tianba, to apprehend the thief. With the help of a friend, Huang Tianba finds out who the real thief is and succeeds in persuading Dou Erdun to return the horse and surrender himself to the authorities. See 201.

204. Hao Wen with a white monk face in *Dongchang Prefecture*, adapted from a story in *Magistrate Shi's Casebook*. Hao Wen is the son of Hao Shihong, an outlaw of Dongchang Prefecture. He has become a monk in the Xuantan Temple, but learning that a cousin of his has been executed by the authorities vows to avenge his death. One day when Magistrate Shi Shilun is passing by the temple, Hao Wen kidnaps him and holds him in his father's house. Law officer Huang Tianba, hearing of this, enters the Hao family's home at night, pretending that he has been engaged to Hao Wen's daughter Suyu. He frees the magistrate and arrests both Hao Wen and his father, but Hao Wen's daughter escapes.

205. Xie Hu with a black-and-blue flowered three-tile face in *Peach Blossom*. Xie Hu is a robber nicknamed 'Peach Blossom,'' who not only robs but rapes and murders. Law officer Huang Tianba is sent to arrest him. He finds the robber in a temple, but is wounded by one of the robber's darts. When his friend Zhu Guangzu arrives to help him, the robber has escaped.

206. Jin Dali with a rubbed-in black full face in *Bala Temple*, adapted from a story in *Magistrate Shi's Casebook*. Fei Degong, a despot, and his henchmen go to the Bala Temple where they abduct a number of local girls. Huang Tianba, a law officer, sees them and devises a plan to arrest them. He has his wife dressed up as a girl burning incense in the temple. True to his expectations, the tyrant abducts her too and takes her to his home where he forces her to marry him. She pretends to agree, but secretly steals his precious sword and the darts he concealed in his sleeves. Huang Tianba and his men arrive, and after a fierce struggle arrest the tyrant. Jin Dali is a friend of Huang Tianba's.

207. Zhu Guangzu with a warrior-clown face in *Chain-Bend Stockade*. He is Huang Tianba's friend and helper.

208. Pu Dayong with a red broken-flower face, a minor character in *Nine-Dragon Cup*, an opera adapted from a story in *Honorable Peng's Casebook*, a novel of the late Qing. It tells how an official called Peng Peng, revered as the Honorable Peng, checked and solved difficult cases during his inspection tours and how a host of men of chivalry helped him fight local despots. In the opera Emperor Kangxi's nine-dragon cup has been stolen and the emperor orders Huang Santai to solve the case. Huang Santai gives a big banquet, the secret purpose of which is to try to find out who stole the cup. Many greenwood heroes are invited. During the banquet, one of Huang's men deliberately

brags about Huang's courage and skill. This incites Yang Xiangwu, one of the greenwood heroes present, to start bragging about his own exploits. Unaware of the trap, he boasts how he entered the palace and stole the emperor's precious cup.

209. Huang Santai with a pink three-tile face, the leading character in *A Meeting of Heroes,* adapted from a story in *Honorable Peng's Casebook.* Peng Peng, or the Honorable Peng, has been dismissed from office for arresting the wicked son of a local despot. His friend Li Qihou calls together a band of greenwood heroes to discuss how to reinstate him. Huang Santai's son, Huang Tianba, sends Ji Quan around, with a golden dart as token, to borrow money. Dou Erdun refuses to give any money; instead he challenges Huang Santai to a duel. Huang wounds Dou by a secret weapon and the two become enemies. See 203.

210. He Lutong with a yellow broken-flower face in *Fallen Horse Lake.* Magistrate Shi Shilun is kidnapped by bandits, who turn him over to Li Pei, bandit chief at Fallen Horse Lake. Li Pei wants to kill him, but his son, Li Dacheng, who has once been generously treated by the magistrate, resolves to save him. To gain time, he suggests to his father that the magistrate be executed in a ceremony honoring greenwood heroes who died at his hands. When his father assents, he hides the magistrate in a cave, then secretly sends word of his whereabouts to Huang Tianba. Huang and He Lutong, another law officer, sneak in and free the magistrate; and He Lutong arrests the bandit chief after a scuffle in the lake.

211. Huang Longji with a blue flowered pointed three-tile face in *The Overlord's Village.* The head of Huangliang Village, he attempts to assassinate Magistrate Shi Shilun and is arrested by Huang Tianba.

212. Ba Yongtai with a red pointed three-tile face in *Chain-Bend Stockade.* He is a subordinate of Liang Jiugong, a high-ranking military officer (see 203). On the latter's orders, he dispatches Huang Tianba to arrest the man who stole the imperial steed.

213. Jiao Zhenyuan with a blue pointed three-tile face, a bandit chief in *Sword-Peak Mountain,* adapted from a story in a sequel to *Honorable Peng's Casebook.* Jiuhua Niang (literally "Mistress Nine Flowers"), owner of a wine and tea shop, is a seductive woman who has lured many men to their destruction. When soldiers come to arrest her, she flees to Sword-Peak Mountain where Jiao Zhenyuan has his stronghold. The soldiers give chase and meet a man called Sheng Kui on the way. The man says he is an old friend of the bandit chief, and volunteers to go and persuade him to give up the fugitive. However, when he arrives at the mountain stronghold and explains the purpose of his visit, his words provoke the bandit chief who not only refuses to grant his request but threatens to kill him. Only the intercession of the bandit's wife saves Sheng Kui's life. The latter now goes to Qiu Cheng, a sworn brother of his, to ask for help. Although Jiao Zhenyuan has always feared Qiu Cheng, he still refuses to give up Jiuhua Niang. Therefore, Qiu Cheng calls together some of his friends and with the help of government soldiers they storm the bandit stronghold, capturing both the bandit chief and the woman.

214. Hua Delei with a white pointed three-tile face in *Xihuang Village.* Hua Delei, a despot of Xihuang Village, and Yin Liang, a thief and rapist, are friends and collaborators in numerous crimes. When Peng Peng, or the Honorable Peng, makes a private visit to the

village, he is recognized by the two, who kidnap him and imprison him in a dungeon. Peng's men together with their wives and daughters enter the village disguised as street performers. They rescue Peng and arrest the despot.

215. Wu Tianqiu with a green broken-flower face, a bandit chief in *Fierce Tiger Village*. In order to avenge the deaths of some of his companions, he kidnaps Magistrate Shi Shilun when the latter is passing through the village on his way to his new post at Jiangdu. Law officer Huang Tianba arrives, learns what has happened, and returns with soldiers who burn the bandit chief's stronghold and rescue the magistrate.

216. Li Pei with a purple pointed three-tile face, bandit chief of Fallen Horse Lake in the opera of the same name.

217. Cai Tianhua with a white flowered three-tile face in *Huai'an Prefecture*. Cai is a bandit disguised as the chief priest of the North Pole Taoist Temple in Huai'an Prefecture. Learning that Magistrate Shi Shilun has arrived at the prefecture, he goes to the prefectural office and steals the magistrate's seal, hiding it in the temple. Law officer Huang Tianba looks for it everywhere in vain. Finally, He Renjie, son of Huang's sworn brother, finds out where the seal is. He steals it back and together with Huang and others captures Cai Tianhua.

218. Deng Jiugeng with a pink three-tile face, a chivalrous old man in *Sister 13*, adapted from the novel *Heroic Sons and Daughters* by Wen Kang of the Qing dynasty. Ji Xiantang, a high-ranking general, sees the beautiful daughter of one of his subordinates and wants to marry her. When her father refuses, the enraged general kills him. To escape the wrath of the general, the daughter, called Yufeng,

and her mother flee from their home. The general dispatches an officer called Bao Chenggong to assassinate them, but Yufeng who is a skilled fighter overpowers the would-be assassin. Instead of killing the man, she pardons him. Moved by the girl's leniency, Bao Chenggong tells her that a knight errant called Deng Jiugong, who is always ready to help the oppressed, lives nearby. She and her mother go to Deng Jiugong, who accepts the girl as his disciple and expresses willingness to help them. Yufeng changes her name to Sister 13 and goes into hiding to await an opportunity to avenge her father's death.

219. Lang Rubao with an old gray three-tile face in *Black-Sea Dock*. A despot of Shandong Province, Lang murders a girl who refuses to marry him, then steals Magistrate Shi Shilun's seal. Huang Tianba recovers the seal and brings the despot to justice.

220. Dou Hu with a twisted yellow face, hatchet man of the tyrant Fei Degong in *Bala Temple*. See 204.

221. God of Wealth with a red fairy face, a celestial being in the opera *Bestowal of Grace*, also called *Heavenly Official Bestows Grace*. It tells how a heavenly creature, on the orders of the Jade Emperor of Heaven and accompanied by the Stars of Emolument and Longevity and by gods of wealth, goes down to earth to dispense gifts to all good people. Considered an auspicious play, it is often the first number in an opera program.

222. Kang Jinlong, or Kang the Golden Dragon, with a black symbolic face, a celestial creature in the opera *Pipa Cave*. The monk Sanzang is captured by a scorpion she-monster who lives in Pipa Cave. She wants the monk to marry her. Sanzang's disciples Monkey and Pigsy fight the scorpion and are badly stung. Finally, calling on the help of Ang'ri Ji, a celestial

rooster, and Kang Jinlong, a dragon, they subdue the scorpion and rescue Sanzang. This opera is adapted from an episode in *Pilgrimage to the West,* a novel by Wu Cheng'en (1510?-1582?) of the Ming dynasty that is based on popular tales, poetic dramas, and storytellers' scripts about Monk Sanzang's pilgrimage to India in quest of Buddhist scriptures. Written in the style of Chinese romantic literature, the novel is rich in imagination, humorous in language, and full of intriguing events. It has provided an inexhaustible supply of source material for Chinese operas and other performing arts.

223. Ling Guan with a red fairy face, a supernatural being in *Sizhou City,* also called *Presenting a Pearl at Rainbow Bridge.* The opera is about a mother jellyfish who lives in an underwater crystal palace at Rainbow Bridge near Sizhou City. Having spent a thousand years in religious meditation, she has acquired supernatural powers but still longs for secular joys. One day she sees the handsome son of the magistrate of Sizhou. By her magical powers she brings him to her underwater palace and forces him to marry her. He tricks her into giving him a pearl with which he can travel safely through water; then he intoxicates her and flees. When the monster awakes and finds the young man gone, she floods Sizhou City. Gods come to the rescue of the city but none is her match. Finally, Guanyin the Goddess of Mercy arrives and by a series of tricks succeeds in shackling the monster. This opera is based on a story from *Casual Talks on the Chou-E,* a novel about the notorious eunuch Wei Zhongxian (1568-1627) and political life in the late Ming. Chou-E is a mythical beast often used in ancient Chinese fables as an allegory of a very wicked person.

224. Ang'ri Ji with a red symbolic bird's face, a celestial rooster in *Pipa Cave.* see 222.

225. Jade Emperor with a silver three-tile fairy face in *Bimawen.* The Jade Emperor is the ruler of Heaven in the novel *Pilgrimage to the West.* Afraid of the Monkey King, he tries to bring him under control by conferring on him the title of *bimawen,* which is actually only a groom. When Monkey learns the truth, he raises hell in the imperial stable and then wreaks havoc all over Heaven.

226. Li the Heavenly King with a red pointed three-tile fairy face. His name is Li Jing and he is also called Li the Pagoda-Bearing Heavenly King. In the opera *Havoc in Heaven,* he is sent by the Jade Emperor with a host of heavenly soldiers to arrest the Monkey King.

227. Sakyamuni with a gold fairy face in *The True and False Monkey Kings.* At one point in his journey to India, the monk Sanzang is waylaid by a band of robbers. Monkey kills them all, but Sanzong accuses him of being too cruel and sends him away. After Monkey leaves, a six-eared macaque posing as Monkey comes and steals Sanzang's belongings. Guanyin the Goddess of Mercy sends Monkey back to subdue the impostor, but the two monkeys are so alike that no one, in Heaven or on Earth, can tell which is the real Monkey King. Finally, the two are brought before Sakyamuni Buddha who sees through the macaque's disguise and exposes him. Before he can escape, Monkey strikes him down with his gold-hooped rod.

228. The Great Sage, the Equal of Heaven, with a red symbolic face, the central character in *Havoc in Heaven,* based on one of the most famous episodes in *Pilgrimage to the West.* The Monkey King has been given the title "The Great Sage, the Equal of Heaven" and is ordered to guard the Peach Garden. One day he learns from some fairy girls picking peaches

in the garden that a peach banquet is being held at Jade Pond, but he has not been invited. In a rage, he rushes to the pond, helps himself to the peaches and fairy wine, then makes his way to a palace where he swallows some pills of immortality. Heavenly generals and soldiers are sent to arrest him, but he defeats them all and storms out of Heaven through the south gate.

229. Zhao the Heavenly Sovereign with a black flowered six-tenth face, a military god of wealth and one of the four heavenly kings in *Havoc in Heaven.*

230. Wen the Heavenly Sovereign with a green broken-flower face, one of the four heavenly kings in *Havoc in Heaven..*

231. Ma the Heavenly Sovereign, also called Ma the King, with a white flowered three-tile face, one of the four heavenly kings in *Havoc in Heaven.*

232. Liu the Heavenly Sovereign with a red three-tile face, one of the four heavenly kings in *Havoc in Heaven.*

233. Monster Spirit with a black flowered ingot face, captain of Li the Heavenly King's vanguard in *Havoc in Heaven.* See 226.

234. Blue Dragon with a blue symbolic face, the eastern god of war and a personified constellation in *Havoc in Heaven.*

235. Erlang God with a golden three-tile fairy face, the Jade Emperor's nephew who is sent to arrest Monkey Sun Wukong in *Havoc in Heaven.* Skilled in magic transformation and aided by a fierce dog, he proves himself the equal of the formidable Monkey King.

236. White Tiger with a white symbolic face, the western god of war and a personified constellation in *Havoc in Heaven.*

237. Monkey Luo with a tile-gray symbolic face, a heavenly warrior and personified constellation in *Havoc in Heaven.*

238. Black Monkey with a black symbolic face, one of the monkeys on Flower-and-Fruit Mountain in *Restoring Peace in Heaven.*

239. Gibbon with a red symbolic face in *Birth of the Stone Monkey,* adapted from an episode in *Pilgrimage to the West* that tells how Monkey Sun Wukong, or the Monkey King, was born. Gibbon is a wise old ape. He advises Monkey Sun Wukong to learn Taoism. Monkey goes to the Kunlun Mountains and there meets a supernatural being who teaches him the 72 metamorphoses and how to somersault through the clouds. He returns and strangles the Devil King who occupied his home in Flower-and-Fruit Mountain during his absence.

240. White Ape with a white symbolic face, the leading character in *Eight Immortals Fight the White Ape,* an opera adapted from a fairy tale. The Queen of Heaven hosts a banquet at Jade Pond. White Ape comes in and steals some of the wine and fairy peaches, whereupon the queen orders the Eight Immortals to drive him away. Later, learning that the ape stole the peaches to cure his old mother's illness, she relents and gives him the fruit.

241. Dipper God with a blue fairy face in *Restoring Peace in Heaven,* one of the 28 personified constellations in *Pilgrimage to the West.*

242. Killer God with a black flowered ingot face in *Imperial Banquet,* an opera adapted from the novel *Three Chivalrous and Five Righteous.* Ge Dengyun, a retired tutor of the emperor, abducts the wife of scholar Fan Zhongyu. When the scholar learns of the whereabouts of his wife, he goes to Ge Dengyun's house and demands her release. Ge pretends to know nothing about the abduction. He offers the scholar wine and, when the latter is drunk, orders a henchman to murder him. But Killer God arrives and kills the would-be murderer

first.

243. God of the Earth with a black fairy face, a personified constellation in *Restoring Peace in Heaven*.

244. Thunder God with a blue symbolic bird's face, a warrior in *Havoc in Heaven* whose weapon is the thunder.

245. Bull Monster with a golden symbolic face, one of the leading characters in *The Palm-leaf Fan*, adapted from an episode in *Pilgrimage to the West*. Monk Sanzang and his disciples arrive at the foot of a flaming mountain which they are unable to cross. They are told that Princess Iron Fan has a palm-leaf fan that can extinguish the flames, so Monkey goes to the princess to borrow the fan. Princess Iron Fan is the wife of a bull monster who was once Monkey's friend but is now his enemy. When he refuses to give them the fan, Monkey calls on soldiers from Heaven to help him. They subdue the monster, take the fan, and cross the mountain safely.

246. Pigsy Bajie with a rubbed-in black symbolic face, the leading character in *Old Gao's Village*. Pigsy is a monster. He transforms himself into a human being and marries Landlord Gao's daughter. When the monk Sanzang and Monkey Sun Wukong pass through the village on their way to the west, Monkey subdues Pigsy and makes him a second disciple of Sanzang. Sanzang gives him the religious name Bajie.

247. Sandy Wujing with a blue monk face in *The River of Shifting Sands*. Sandy is a water monster who lives in this river. When Sanzang and his two discipales, Monkey and Pigsy, arrive at the river, Monkey with the help of the Goddess of Mercy makes Sandy a third disciple of the monk. He is given the religious name Wujing.

248. Yellow-robed Monster with a yellow symbolic face, a character in the *Kingdom of Precious Elephants*. The monster is one of the 28 constellations personified in *Pilgrimage to the West*. He has secretly come down to earth to seek worldly joys and, meeting Monk Sanzang and his disciples, kidnaps the monk. The monster's wife is a princess of the Kingdom of Precious Elephants, who has been abducted by the monster and forced to marry him. She takes pity on the monk and implores her husband to release him. When the monster assents, she writes a letter to her father and secretly gives it to the monk. Learning of the whereabouts of his daughter, the king begs Sanzang's disciples Pigsy and Sandy to rescue her. Monkey has been sent away by Sanzang because of a misunderstanding over the killing of the White-Bone Demon, but now Pigsy persuades him to come back. Together they vanquish the Yellow-robed Monster and escort the princess back to her kingdom.

249. Green Lion with a green symbolic face, a monster in *Lion-and-Camel Ridge*. When Sanzang and his disciples arrive at Lion-and-Camel Ridge, they are stopped by a green lion, a white elephant, and a roc. Monkey subdues the lion and elephant, but is tricked by the roc which captures and imprisons Sanzang. At the request of Monkey, the Buddha arrives and subdues the three monsters.

250. Cat God with a white symbolic face in *The Bottomless Pit*. Sanzang is captured by the White Mouse Spirit, which tries to make him marry her. To rescue his master, Monkey steals a divine tablet with which he summons soldiers from Heaven to help him, but all are powerless. Finally, he calls on the Cat God, which subdues the mouse spirit.

251. White Elephant with a white symbolic face, one of three monsters in *Lion-and-Camel Ridge*.

252. Gold-Coin Leopard with a golden symbolic

face in *Red Plum Mountain*. The leopard is a monster which has occupied Red Plum Mountain and wants to marry the daughter of the local squire. When Sanzang and his disciples arrive at the mountain, Monkey tries to subdue the monster, but it holds out until soldiers from Heaven arrive and overpower it.

253. Peacock with a green symbolic face, a supernatural in *Hundred-Grass Mountain,* an opera based on a legend *The Lotus in the Alms Bowl.* A she-monster of Hundred-Grass Mountain transforms herself into a woman and goes to Wang Family Village with a magic bowl as weapon. The Goddess of Mercy, hearing of this, sends an earth god to the village disguised as a pot mender. The monster comes to him with her bowl and asks him to mend it, but he deliberately drops and breaks it, depriving the monster of her weapon. The Goddess now sends Peacock together with a roc, a parrot, and other heavenly warriors to the village and they exterminate the monster.

254. Daytime Parrort with a white symbolic face, a fairy bird in *Hundred-Grass Mountain.*

255. Tongque Bird with a red symbolic face, a fairy bird in *Hundred-Grass Mountain.*

256. Roc with a green symbolic face, a monster in *Lion-and-Camel Ridge.* A guardian of the law at the Buddha's side, it sneaks away to make trouble on earth but is captured and brought back by the Buddha.

257. Ao Guang with an old white three-tile face, the dragon king of the East Sea in *Water-Curtain Cave,* adapted from an episode in *Pilgrimage to the West.* When Monkey begins practicing the martial arts in his Water-Curtain Cave, he finds he is in need of a good weapon. He goes to Ao Guang, the dragon king, who gives him a magic needle with power to calm the seas. Monkey is pleased to get this weapon but wants the king to give him helmets and armor as well. Seeing that Monkey is asking for more and more, the king calls together his dragon brothers, generals, and soldiers to drive him out. They are defeated by Monkey who runs riot in the dragon palace.

258. Lobster general with a demon's face, an aquatic creature in the dragon king's palace in *Water-Curtain Cave.*

259. Ao Run with an old gray three-tile face, one of the four dragon kings who rule the four seas in *Water-Curtain Cave.*

260. Commander Turtle with a demon's face, an aquatic creature in the dragon king's palace in *Water-Curtain Cave.*

261. The Big Dipper with a purple three-tile face, a personified constellation in *Restoring Peace in Heaven.*

262. Han Zhongli with a red fairy face, one of the eight immortals in *Eight Immortals Cross the Sea,* an opera based on a Chinese fairy tale.

263. Willow Spirit with a green-gold broken-flower face, a disciple of Lü Dongbin, one of the immortals in *Eight Immortals Cross the Sea.*

264. Jade Hare with a white symbolic face, Lady Chang'e's pet in *Chang'e Flees to the Moon.* It accompanied the lady in her flight to the moon palace.

265. Toad Spirit with a green symbolic face in *Five-Flower Cave,* an opera based on a Chinese fairy tale. In China, the toad, lizard, scorpion, snake, and centipede are called the five poisons. In the opera the five after undergoing a period of self-cultivation acquire supernatural powers. They leave for the country's capital, intending to make trouble there, but are overpowered by a god called Zhang Jie.

266. Golden-Head Spirit with a blue-and-gold symbolic face in *Five-Flower Cave.* This spirit is a centipede turned monster and is the

ringleader of the poisonous five.

267. The Dog That Barks at Heaven with a white symbolic face, companion of Erlang God in *Restoring Peace in Heaven*.

268. Scorpion Spirit with a green symbolic face in *Five-Flower Cave*.

269. Wei Tuo with a golden fairy face in *The Closed Bowl*, adapted from *The Legend of Leifeng Pagoda*. A white snake and a green snake, tired of practicing meditation in the Emei Mountains, transform themselves into two girls called Bai Suzhen ("White Maid") and Xiao Qing. They go to beautiful West Lake in Hangzhou and there meet a young man called Xu Xian. Bai Suzhen and Xu Xian fall in love and are married. They take up residence at the home of Xu Xian's brother-in-law, where Bai gives birth to a child. Their happiness, however, is cut short by Fahai, a wicked abbot of the Jinshan Temple, who comes along with Wei Tuo, a supernatural guardian of the Buddhist law. They insist that the couple's hour of parting has come and what fate has ordained cannot be reversed. They clasp Bai Suzhen in a magic alms bowl and imprison her under Leifeng Pagoda. *The Legend of Leifeng Pagoda*, a play of the Qing dynasty, is based on a folk tale about a white snake transformed into a girl, who becomes an example of loyalty (to her true love), courage (in resisting feudal oppression), and self-sacrifice, Fahai the abbot exemplifies the evils of feudalism.

270. Deer Child with a green symbolic face, a fairy in *Stealing the Magic Herb*, adapted from an episode in *The Legend of Leifeng Pagoda*. On the Dragon-Boat Festival one year, Xu Xian (see 269) offers his wife, the White Maid, some realgar wine. Unable to resist her husband's persuasion, she drinks a bit too much and is transformed back into a white snake. Her husband drops dead from fright, and she hurries to the Kunlun Mountains to steal a magic herb to revive him. Two guardians of the mountains, Deer Child and Crane Child, discover her but she fights them off. They report to their master, Old Fairy of the South Pole, who comes and arrests the girl. But when he learns why she is here, he takes pity on her and gives her some of the life-restoring herb, with which she returns and revives her husband.

271. Taiyi the Immortal with a red three-tile fairy face in *Heavenly Mountain*, adapted from an episode in *Canonization of the Gods*. Taiyi is a god in Chinese mythology. In some ancient writings, he is identified as the supreme god or ruler of Heaven. In this opera Nezha, a disciple of his, goes out to practice archery one day and accidently kills the servant maid of Shiji, a rock fairy. Shiji pursues Nezha to Heavenly Mountain where Nezha begs Taiyi to come out and save him. Taiyi tries to mediate between the two, but Shiji insists that Nezha must pay for the accidental killing with his life. Her stubbornness angers Taiyi, who engulfs her in a fire and transforms her into rock.

272. Crane Child with a white symbolic face in *Stealing the Magic Herb*. He and Deer Child are the two guardians of the Kunlun Mountains.

中國歷史年代簡表
A Brief Chronology of Chinese History

夏 Xia (c.2100-c.1600 B.C.)	西魏 Western Wei (535-557)
商 Shang (c.1600-c.1027 B.C.)	北齊 Northern Qi (550-577)
周 Zhou (c.1027-256 B.C.)	北周 Northern Zhou (557-581)
西周 Western Zhou (c.1027-771 B.C.)	南朝 Southern Dynasties (420-589)
東周 Eastern Zhou (770-256 B.C.)	宋 Song (420-479)
春秋 Spring & Autumn (770-476 B.C.)	齊 Qi (479-502)
戰國 Warring States (475-221 B.C.)	梁 Liang (502-557)
秦 Qin (221-207 B.C.)	陳 Chen (557-589)
漢 Han (206 B.C.-220 A.D.)	隋 Sui (581-618)
西漢 Western Han (206 B.C.-8 A.D.)	唐 Tang (618-907)
新 Xin (9-23)	五代 Five Dynasties (907-960)
東漢 Eastern Han (25-220)	宋 Song (960-1279)
三國 Three Kingdoms (220-265)	北宋 Northern Song (960-1127)
魏 Wei (220-265)	南宋 Southern Song (1127-1279)
蜀 Shu (221-263)	遼 Liao (916-1125)
吳 Wu (222-280)	金（女真）Jin (Jurchen) (1115-1234)
晉 Jin (265-420)	元 Yuan (1271-1368)
西晉 Western Jin (265-317)	北元 Northern Yuan (1370-1403)
東晉 Eastern Jin (317-420)	明 Ming (1368-1644)
南北朝 Northern and Southern Dynasties (420-589)	南明 Southern Ming (1644-1661)
北朝 Northern Dynasties (386-581)	清 Qing (1636-1911)
北魏 Northern Wei (386-534)	後金 Later Jin (Jurchen) (1616-1636)
東魏 Eastern Wei (534-550)	

註：三國的吳，東晉，南朝的宋、齊、梁、陳，都以建康（吳名建業，今江蘇南京）為首都。歷史上合稱六朝，是公元三世紀初到六世紀末前後 300 餘年的歷史時期的泛稱。

Note: The Wu of the Three Kingdoms, the Eastern Jin, and the Song, Qi, Liang and Chen of the Southern Dynasties, all of which had their capitals in what is now Nanjing, Jiangsu Province, are collectively known as the **Six Dynasties**. They span a period of more than 300 years, between the early third century and the late sixth century AD.

编辑和装帧设计：孙　杰
摄　　影：吴寅伯、张祖道
英文翻译：龚理曾
英文核稿：王行正
技术编辑：于深泉

京 剧 脸 谱

朝华出版社编

出版者：朝华出版社
（中国国际图书贸易总公司出版机构）
中国北京车公庄西路 35 号
印刷者：强华印刷厂

发行者：中国国际图书贸易总公司
（中国国际书店）
中国北京车公庄西路 35 号
邮政编码：100044
中国北京第399号信箱

787×1092毫米1/16开本　　9 印张
1992年第一版　　1992年第一次印刷
1994年第一版 第二次印刷
ISBN7－5054－0412－1/J·0132
84-E-652p　　　04800